COMMON WILD FLOWERS OF MINNESOTA

Common
WILD FLOWERS
of Minnesota

ILLUSTRATIONS BY WILMA MONSERUD

TEXT BY GERALD B. OWNBEY

University of Minnesota Press, Minneapolis

Table of Contents

Library of Congress Catalog Card Number: 72-161439

ISBN 0-8166-0609-9

List of Illustrations

Dicotyledonae. Dicotyledons

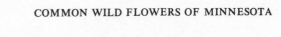

COMMON WILD FLOWERS OF MINNESOTA

Introduction

THIS book was prepared as a guide for the general public, teachers, and students at the pre-college level in the identification of the common wild flowers in Minnesota. It should prove particularly useful to those persons who have an interest in natural history but do not have the time or resources for extensive formal training in this field and to those who wish to learn the names of familiar flowers before engaging in more specialized studies.

Every effort was made to ensure that the drawings are accurate so that direct comparisons can be made with the living plants. Detailed drawings of parts, when given, portray the features of the plant that are most useful in determining its identity with certainty. Whenever possible, the drawings of the plants are life size and in all instances the magnification of the drawing is given.

Within the boundaries of Minnesota there are about 1800 species of flowering plants known to exist in the wild state. Including all of these species would produce a volume too bulky to be practical. Therefore, we have selected about 300 of the herbs that are most common and conspicuous, at least when in flower. Most of them are found over large sections of the state. Woody plants are excluded as are grasses and most grasslike plants. Several attractive plants not native to the United States are included because they have become naturalized and are self-perpetuating outside cultivation.

Supplementary information about each plant includes the color of the petals, the flowers or flower clusters, and the stature when not self-evident from the drawing. The habitat is described in general terms and the area of the state where the species is found is delimited. The primary source of information used in determining the distribution of each species was the collection of preserved specimens in the herbarium of the University of Minnesota. These specimens have been assembled over a period of about 80 years and represent the most complete documentation, from past to present, of the flora of the state to be found anywhere. Because of the displacement of the native vegetation by agriculture during this time period, the distributions based upon preserved specimens are not absolutely correct today. Also, studies of

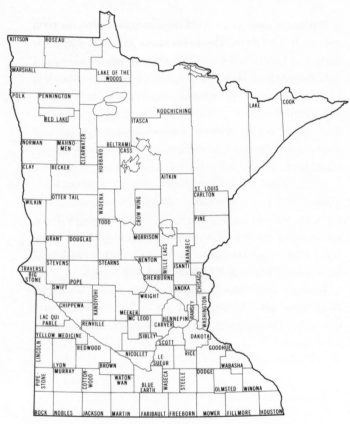

County Map of Minnesota

the state flora are continuing and new information about species distribution is still being compiled.

In the prairie areas of the southern and western parts of the state, which are most suitable for intensive farming, the native flora persists only in preserves and in secluded pockets along river bluffs, railroads, and so forth. Even in pastures that have not been plowed but have been subjected to grazing by domesticated animals for several decades, the composition of the plant cover has changed notably. In the coniferous and deciduous forest zones, however, there are still sizable tracts in which the native flora is still largely intact. Probably no plant species has been exterminated in Minnesota in modern times, but several have become extremely rare.

All of the species illustrated in this book belong to the Angiospermae or angiosperms, a group which encompasses all of the flowering plants. The angiosperms are divided into 2 major groups, the Monocotyledonae or monocotyledons which include the orchids, lilies, and allied plants and the Dicotyledonae or dicotyledons, by far the larger one, which include the remainder of the flowering plants. The separation of the monocotyledons from the dicotyledons is maintained within this book and the families under each one are alphabetically arranged by their Latin names.

Under each family the genera are also alphabetically arranged by their Latin names as are the species of each genus, in the most instances. This sequence, although completely arbitrary, does make each illustration easy to find by persons unfamiliar with the classification system used by professionals in plant systematics. Also, an index to both the common and the Latin names appears at the back of the book.

The term species used upon occasion throughout the text has no exact equivalent in everyday language. In many instances it means approximately the same as kind or variety, but it is more precise. Most people, for example, can readily recognize several different kinds of orchids such as the yellow lady-slipper, the moccasin flower, and the showy orchis. Botanically speaking, these kinds of orchids are also species as are many of the other sorts of wild flowers that most people can distinguish. However, in many instances, a single kind of flower may include several botanical species or several kinds may be grouped together under a single botanical species. To avoid these complications, the term species is used here. The Latin name for each species is given in addition to the common name to establish, beyond doubt, the botanical species under discussion. Unavoidably, in different parts of the state or country, the same common name may be used for different species or the same species may have several common names. Each botanical species, on the other hand, has only one correct Latin name the world over.

For the most part, words used to describe the plants, their parts, and their various other attributes have been drawn from the vernacular. Sometimes, for reasons of clarity or precision, it has been necessary to adopt a technical term. All of these terms are defined and sometimes are illustrated in the glossary to be found at the back of the book.

We hope our efforts in preparing this book will benefit and provide many hours of pleasure for the readers. If this is the case, the artist and the author will feel fully compensated.

Monocotyledonae

THIS group of flowering plants is commonly termed the monocotyledons or monocots for short. Its members usually have the main veins of the leaves parallel, that is, all of the main veins extend from the base to the tip of the leaf blade. Usually there are 3 flower parts of each kind in a single flower, that is, 3 sepals, petals, stamens, and carpels or, in some instances, the parts occur in multiples of 3. The embryonic plant within the seed normally has 1 seed leaf or cotyledon. Other equally important features of the group are found in the internal structure of the stem.

ALISMATACEAE. *Water-plantain Family*

WATER-PLANTAIN (*Alisma plantago-aquatica*).

1. Habit, x ⅛. 2. Basal leaf, x ⅓. 3. Inflorescence, x ⅓. 4. Flower, x 3. 5. Fruit cluster from beneath, x 3. 6. Fruit cluster from above, x 3. 7. Face view of achene, x 6. 8. Side view of achene, x 6.

Petals white; achenes or "seeds" wedge-shaped, in a wheel-like cluster. Muddy banks along streams or in shallow, quiet water around lakes. Throughout Minnesota.

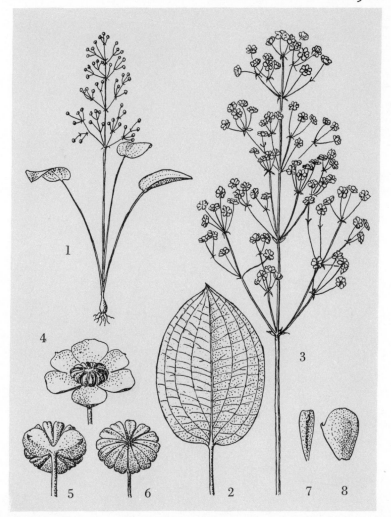

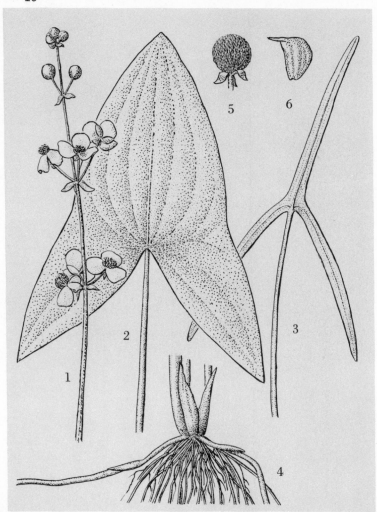

1   2   3   4   5   6

ALISMATACEAE. Water-plantain Family

ARROWHEAD; DUCK-POTATO; WAPATO (*Sagittaria latifolia*).

1. Inflorescence, x ½. 2–3. Typical leaves showing extremes in variation, x ½. 4. Base of plants showing roots and stolons, x ½. 5. Fruit cluster, x 1. 6. Side view of achene, x 2.

Petals white; achenes or "seeds" in a spherical cluster. In shallow water, sloughs, lakeshores, and streams. Throughout Minnesota.

AMARYLLIDACEAE. *Amaryllis Family*

STAR-GRASS (*Hypoxis hirsuta*).

1. Habit, x ½. 2. Bud and flower, x 2. 3. Mature fruit; parts of flower still attached, x 2.

Sepals and petals yellow. Low prairies. Southern and western Minnesota, south and west of a line connecting Washington, Morrison, Mahnomen, and Roseau counties.

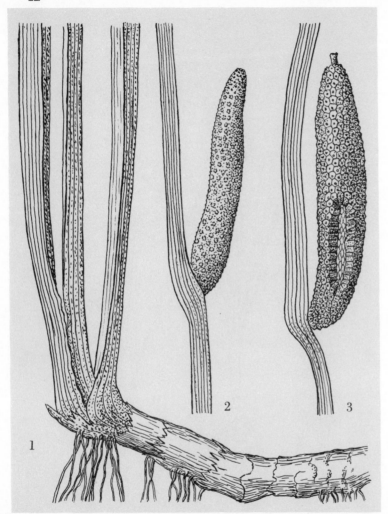

ARACEAE. *Arum Family*

SWEET FLAG (*Acorus calamus*).

1. Base of plant showing rhizome, x 1. 2. Inflorescence at flowering time, x 1. 3. Mature inflorescence; some of the fruits removed, x 1.

Flower clusters greenish, inconspicuous; leaves 1–3 ft. long and about 1 in. wide; sweetly fragrant plant. Marshy meadows or edges of permanent streams. Throughout the state.

ARACEAE. *Arum Family*

JACK-IN-THE-PULPIT (*Arisaema triphyllum*).

1. Habit, x ½. 2. Cluster of mature berries, x 1.
3. Tuber, x 1.

Spathe or "pulpit" from pale green to darkly
striped inside with green and purple, soon wither-
ing; berries red. Low, moist woods. Throughout Minnesota.

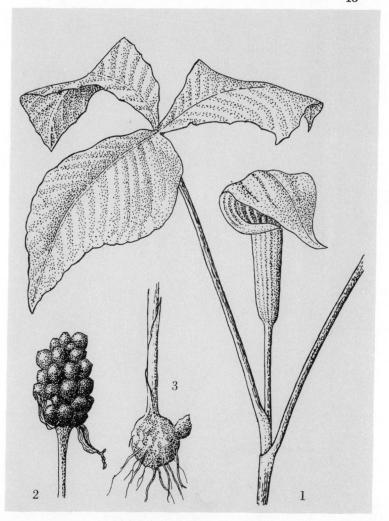

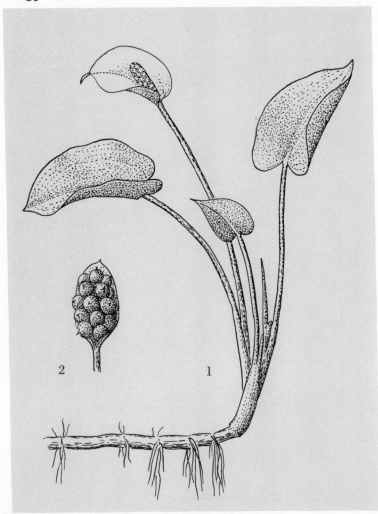

2   1

ARACEAE. *Arum Family*

WATER ARUM (*Calla palustris*).

1. Plant in flower, x ½. 2. Cluster of mature berries, x ½.

Spathe white or greenish; flowers greenish; berries red when ripe. Sedge mats, sloughs, and bogs. Commonest in the northeastern quarter of the state, but found in suitable habitats west to Polk County and south to Le Sueur County.

ARACEAE. Arum Family

SKUNK CABBAGE (*Symplocarpus foetidus*).

The parts of the plant above the surface at flowering time are shown, x 1.

Spathe green or green mottled with darker green or purple, emerging before the leaves. Boggy ground around springs or adjacent to streams. Found in counties near the eastern edge of the state north to Lake County and south to Houston County.

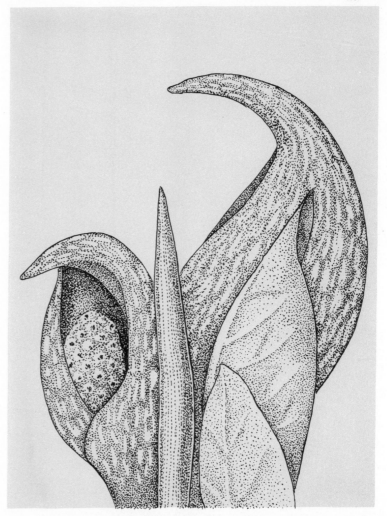

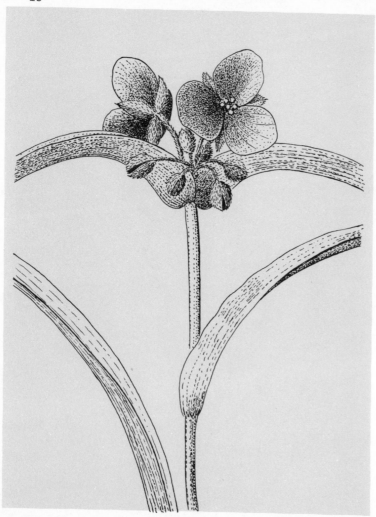

COMMELINACEAE. *Spiderwort Family*

SPIDERWORT (*Tradescantia bracteata*).

The upper parts of the plant at flowering time are shown, x 1.

Petals blue to purple, pink or white, the sepals and pedicels covered with long hairs, some of them with droplets at their tips. Prairies, usually well-drained, sandy areas. Southern and western parts of the state.

COMMELINACEAE. *Spiderwort Family*

SPIDERWORT (*Tradescantia occidentalis*).

The upper parts of the plant at flowering time
are shown, x 1.

Petals blue, sometimes pink, rarely white, the sepals
and pedicels covered with short hairs with droplets
at their tips. Dry prairies. In counties near the Twin
Cities, especially the Anoka Sand Plain, and northwest to Crow Wing County; also Polk, Norman,
and Clay counties.

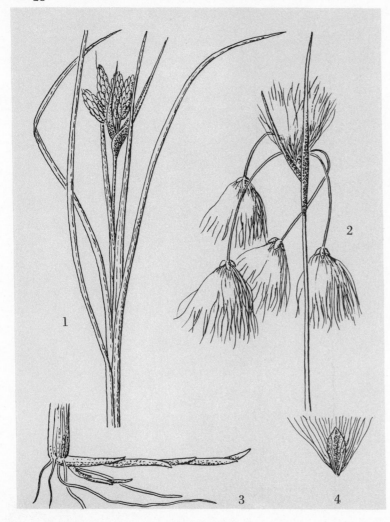

1

2

3

4

CYPERACEAE. *Sedge Family*

COTTON GRASS (*Eriophorum angustifolium*).

1. Upper part of plant before flowering, x 1.
2. Inflorescence in fruit, x 1. 3. Base of plant
showing rhizomes, x 1. 4. Achene or "seed," x 4.

Bristles or "cotton" white or pale yellow. Wet
meadows, swales, roadside ditches, and bogs. Found
generally throughout the state except for the southeastern corner; rare over much of the prairie areas.
Several other cotton grasses occur in Minnesota.
This one is representative.

DIOSCOREACEAE. Yam Family

WILD YAM (*Dioscorea villosa*).

1. Habit, x ½. 2. Mature fruit, x 1. 3. Branch of fruiting inflorescence, x ½. 4. Rhizome, x ½.

Stems twining. Thickets and woods. In counties near the Mississippi River from southern Pine County to Houston County.

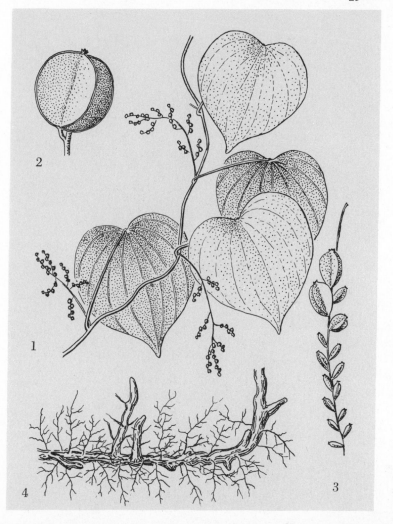

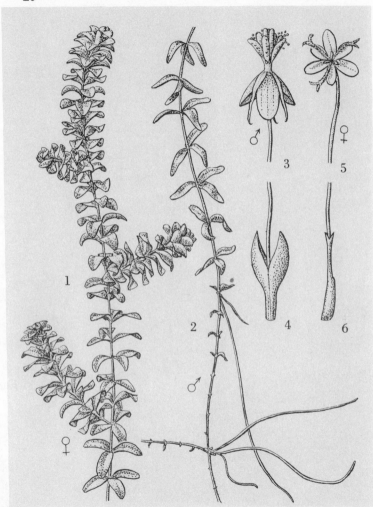

HYDROCHARITACEAE. *Frog's Bit Family*

WATERWEED (*Anacharis canadensis*; *Elodea canadensis*).

1. Habit of female plant, x 1. 2. Habit of male plant, x 1. 3–4. Male flower and associated parts, x 3. 5–6. Female flower and associated parts, x 3.

Found in still waters or slow-moving streams floating in large masses just beneath the surface. Common in the eastern and central parts of the state.

HYDROCHARITACEAE. Frog's Bit Family

TAPEGRASS; EELGRASS; WILD CELERY (*Vallisneria americana*).

1. Base of plant, x ½. 2. Female flower, x 1. 3. Fruit, x 1.

Plants usually growing in 3–5 ft. of water, with only the tips of the leaves reaching the surface; slender stalk of female flowers coiling after pollination. Lakes. Found principally in the eastern half of the state.

IRIDACEAE. *Iris Family*

BLUE FLAG; IRIS (*Iris versicolor*).

Upper part of the plant at flowering time, x 1.

Wet pastures, marshes, swamps, borders of sedge meadows, in full sun. Found over most of the state but less common in the western portion; absent in the southeastern corner. A second species of blue flag, *I. virginica*, is common in wet meadows of the southeastern two-fifths of the state where it largely replaces *I. versicolor*.

IRIDACEAE. *Iris Family*

BLUE-EYED GRASS (*Sisyrinchium campestre*).

1. Habit, x ½. 2. Upper part of the plant, x 1.

Sepals and petals blue, occasionally pale blue or white. Grassy meadows and hillsides, often in sandy soils. Very common throughout the southern half of the state, rare northwestward. One or more of our 4 species of blue-eyed grass occurs in all quarters of the state; all are of similar appearance.

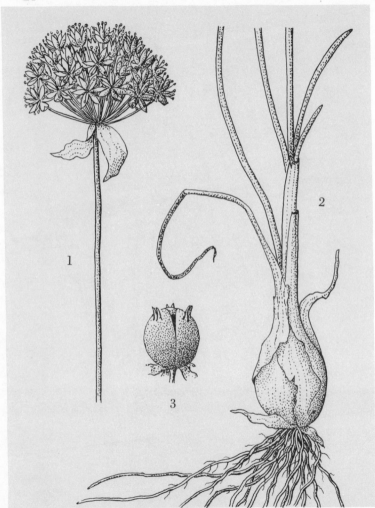

LILIACEAE. Lily Family

WILD ONION (*Allium stellatum*).

1. Inflorescence, x 1. 2. Base of plant showing bulb and roots, x 1. 3. Capsule, x 4.

Sepals and petals pink or rose-colored. In meadows and upland prairies. Throughout the state.

LILIACEAE. Lily Family

WILD ONION (*Allium textile*).

1. Upper part of plant, x 1. 2. Base of plant showing bulb, x 1. 3. Flower, x 2. 4. Capsule, x 4.

Sepals and petals white or pinkish. Dry, upland prairies. Found in a few counties along the western border of Minnesota.

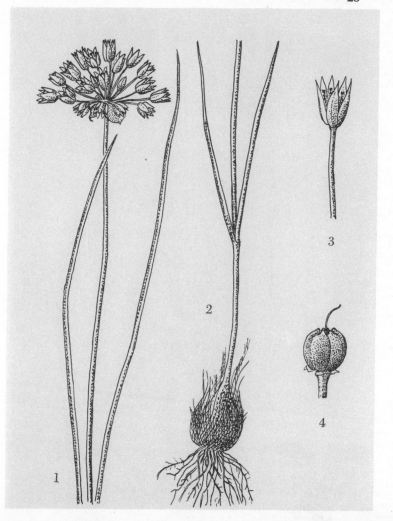

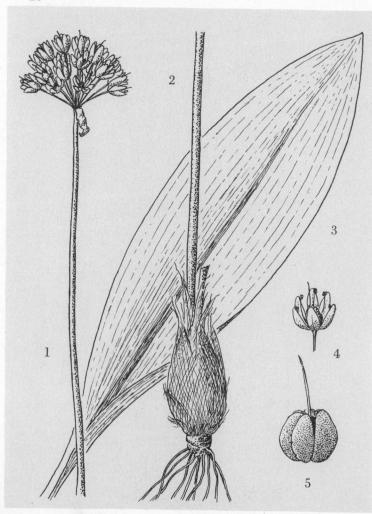

LILIACEAE. Lily Family

WILD LEEK (*Allium tricoccum*).

1. Inflorescence, x 1. 2. Base of plant showing bulb, x 1. 3. Leaf, x 1. 4. Flower, x 2. 5. Capsule, x 4.

Sepals and petals whitish; flowers appearing in the summer, usually after the leaves have died back. Most typically found in mixed hardwood forests, river bottoms, and slopes. Common in the southern half of the state; infrequent farther north.

LILIACEAE. Lily Family

BLUEBEAD LILY; CORY LILY (*Clintonia borealis*).

1. Habit, x ⅓. 2. Flower, x 1. 3. Cluster of berries, x ⅓. 4. Berry, x 1.

Sepals and petals greenish-yellow; berries blue. Moist woods, edges of bogs, etc. Found in the northeastern two-fifths of the state.

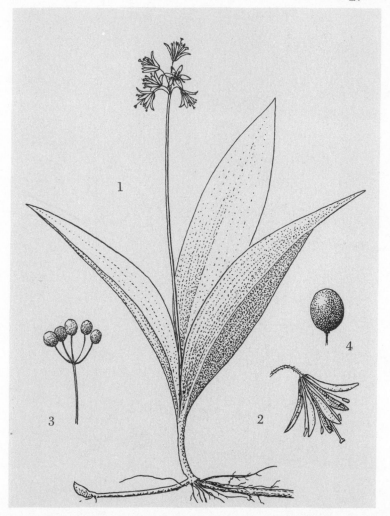

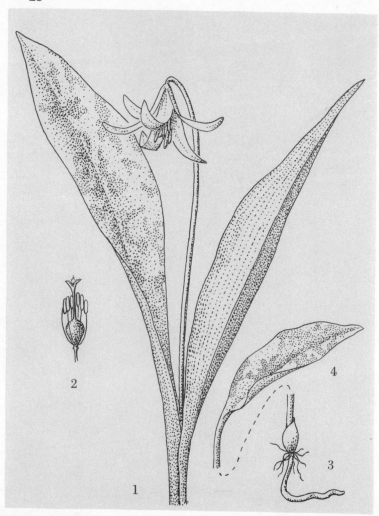

LILIACEAE. Lily Family

WHITE DOG-TOOTH VIOLET; ADDER'S TONGUE; TROUT LILY (*Erythronium albidum*).

1. Habit, x 1. 2. Flower with sepals and petals removed, x 1. 3–4. Young plant with single leaf, bulb, and rhizome, x ½.

Sepals and petals white or pinkish, often suffused with blue on the outside; leaves usually mottled with brown; forming large colonies. Woodlands, the flowers appear before the trees leaf out. Mostly in the southeastern part of the state; occasionally encountered north to St. Louis County. The commonest of our 3 species of dog-tooth violet.

LILIACEAE. *Lily Family*

MICHIGAN TURK'S-CAP LILY (*Lilium michiganense*).

1. Flower, x 1. 2. Central section of flowering stem, x ⅓. 3. Capsule, x 1.

Sepals and petals orange or orange-red spotted with purple; flowers single or frequently in umbels of 2, 3, or more. Found in wet meadows, in full sun. Commonest in the eastern half of the state.

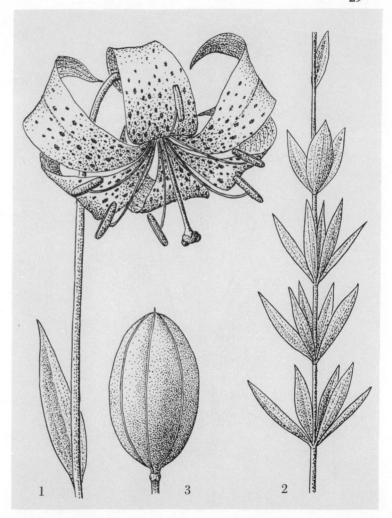

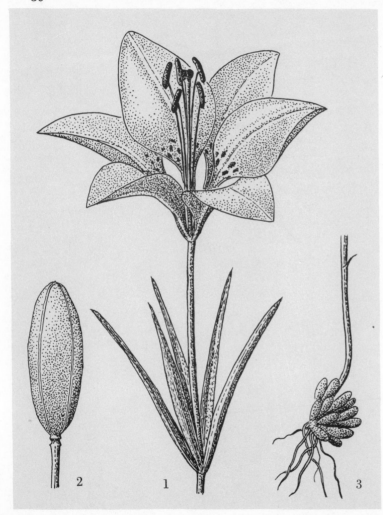

2   1   3

LILIACEAE. Lily Family

WOOD-LILY (*Lilium philadelphicum*).

1. Upper part of stem, x 1. 2. Capsule, x 1.
3. Underground parts, x 1.

Sepals and petals orange to orange-red or yellow,
spotted with purple on the inside; flowers single or
in umbels of 2–5. Moist to dry meadows, thickets,
or in jack pine or red pine forests. Generally
distributed throughout the state.

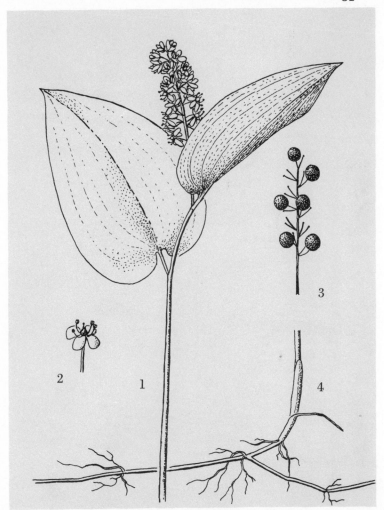

LILIACEAE. Lily Family

WILD OR FALSE LILY-OF-THE-VALLEY (*Maianthemum canadense*).

1. Habit, x 1. 2. Flower, x 2. 3. Mature berries, x 1. 4. Underground parts, x 1.

Flowers white, berries pale red. Spreading extensively by means of underground stems. Growing in semishade at the margins of woods and bogs. Throughout the state except in the western and southern prairies.

1

2

LILIACEAE. *Lily Family*

SOLOMON'S SEAL (*Polygonatum canaliculatum*).
1. Upper part of stem, x ⅓. 2. Berries, x ⅓.

Flowers greenish-white; berries dark blue; stems arching. Woods, partial shade. Mostly in the southern half of the state; uncommon northwestward.

LILIACEAE. *Lily Family*

FALSE SOLOMON'S SEAL (*Smilacina racemosa*).

1. Upper part of stem, x ¼. 2. Flower from side, x 2.
3. Face view of flower with sepals and petals removed,
x 2. 4. Mature berries, x 1.

Flowers white; berries greenish to reddish, flecked
with purple. Spreading from underground stems.
Generally distributed, but less common in the
prairie regions of the state.

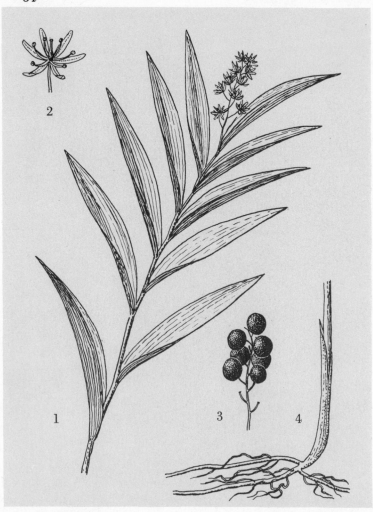

LILIACEAE. *Lily Family*

FALSE SOLOMON'S SEAL (*Smilacina stellata*).

1. Upper part of stem, x ½. 2. Flower, x 2. 3. Mature berries, x ½. 4. Base of plant showing underground parts, x ½.

Flowers white; berries green at first, with dark purple stripes, later turning dark red; extensively spreading from underground stems. Growing in semishade, well-drained soils, open woods, and thickets. Generally distributed throughout the state.

LILIACEAE. *Lily Family*

CARRION-FLOWER (*Smilax herbacea*).

1. Section of stem, x 1. 2. Leaf, x 1. 3. Cluster of berries, x 1.

Flowers pale greenish-yellow, with an unpleasant odor; berries dark blue or black; vines with tendrils. Found in woodlands throughout the state. A second and similar species, *S. ecirrhata*, has the stalks of the flower clusters arising from the axils of bracts below the foliage leaves and frequently lacks the tendrils. The greenbrier, *S. hispida*, a vine with very prickly stems, is also found commonly in woodlands in the southeastern quarter of the state.

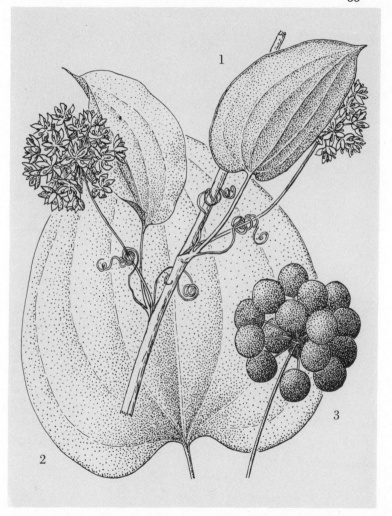

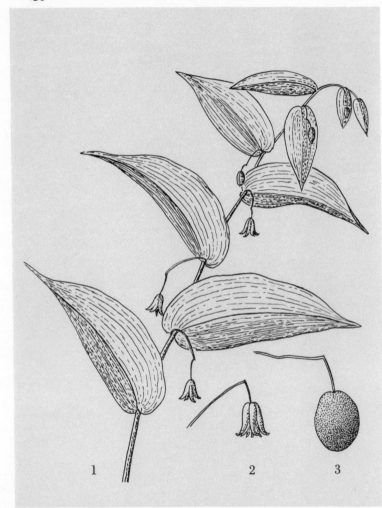

1   2   3

LILIACEAE. Lily Family

TWISTED STALK (*Streptopus amplexifolius*).

1. Upper part of stem, x ½. 2. Flower, x 1.
3. Berry, x 1.

Flowers greenish-white; berries red. Woods. In the Arrowhead region of northeastern Minnesota. *S. roseus*, a more common species than the one illustrated, is found in the central and northeastern parts of the state. It differs in having the leaves stalkless but not deeply heart-shaped at the base and in the greater amount of hair on the stems.

LILIACEAE. Lily Family

FALSE ASPHODEL (*Tofieldia glutinosa*).

1–2. Habit, x 1. 3. Flower, x 2. 4. Capsule, x 2.
5. Seed, x 10.

Sepals and petals whitish. Wet meadows, principally
of filled-in lake beds. Northwestern Minnesota, from
Clearwater to Kittson counties; also reported from
Pope and Hennepin counties.

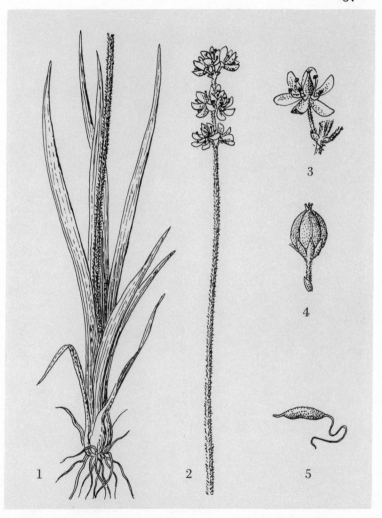

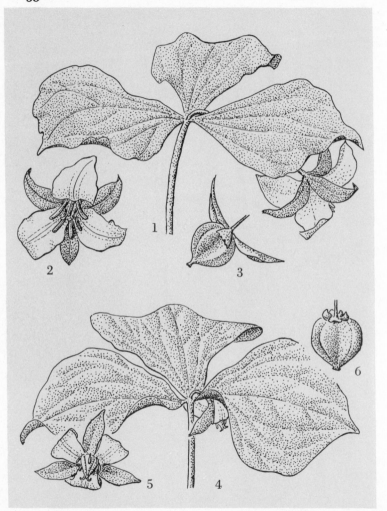

LILIACEAE. Lily Family

DECLINING TRILLIUM (*Trillium flexipes*).

1. Flowering stem, x ½. 2. Flower, x ½.
3. Capsule, x ½.

Petals white; mature berries whitish or tinged with pink, sharply flanged. Moist woods and bottoms. Common in the southeastern fifth of the state, sometimes growing with the next species.

NODDING TRILLIUM; WAKEROBIN (*Trillium cernuum*).

4. Flowering stem, x ½. 5. Flower, x ½.
6. Capsule, x ½.

Petals white, rarely tinged with pink; mature berries usually purplish, nearly globose, with the ridges low. Woods, hillsides, and river bottoms throughout the state.

LILIACEAE. Lily Family

LARGE-FLOWERED TRILLIUM (*Trillium grandiflorum*).

1. Flowering stem, x ½. 2. Capsule, x 1.

Petals white or pink at first, fading to pink or purple in older flowers, the flower stalk erect or nearly so. Open woods, hillsides, and valleys. Most frequent in east-central Minnesota; occasionally seen southeastward and northwestward.

SNOW TRILLIUM (*Trillium nivale*).

3. Flowering stem, x 1. 4. Capsule, x 1.

Petals white, the flower stalk slightly bent at first, more sharply bent later on. Open woods, hillsides, and bottoms. Southeastern Minnesota south of the Minnesota River. Common locally.

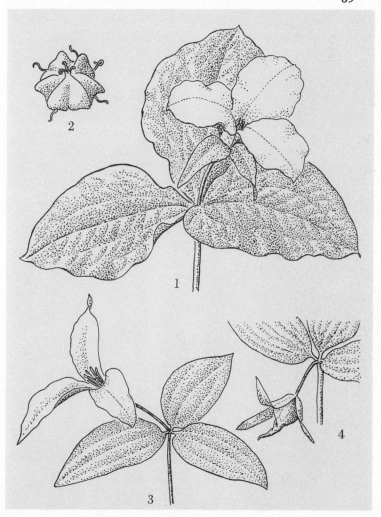

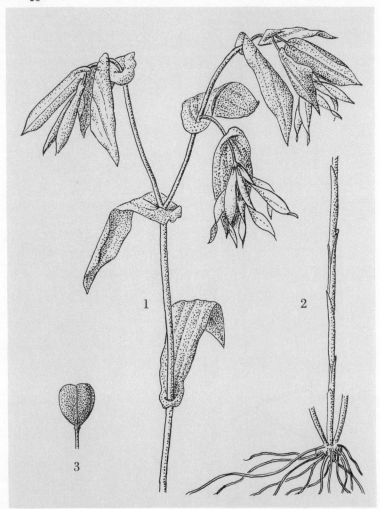

LILIACEAE. Lily Family

BELLWORT (*Uvularia grandiflora*).
1. Flowering stem, x ½. 2. Base of plant, x ½.
3. Capsule, x 1.

Flowers yellow; crowns giving rise to 1 or a few to sometimes numerous stems in clumps. Woods. Found throughout the state, but rare in areas that are predominantly prairie.

LILIACEAE. Lily Family

PALE BELLWORT (*Uvularia sessilifolia*).

1. Upper part of stem, x 1. 2. Middle part of stem, x 1.
3. Base of stem with underground parts attached, x 1.

Flowers pale yellow; forming large colonies by means
of extensive underground stems. Woods. Mostly in
east-central and northeastern Minnesota; rare
westward.

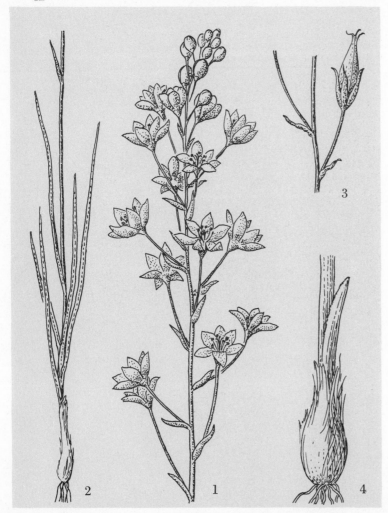

LILIACEAE. Lily Family

WHITE CAMASS (*Zygadenus elegans*).

1. Plant less inflorescence, x ¼. 2. Inflorescence, x 1.
3. Capsule, x 1. 4. Base of stem with bulb, x 1.

Flowers creamy-white, the petals and sepals suffused
on the back with green, brown, or purple; stems
and leaves smooth, bluish; plants poisonous. Moist
to wet prairies or open woods. Found south and west
of a line connecting Winona, Hennepin, Mahnomen,
and Kittson counties.

ORCHIDACEAE. *Orchid Family*

PUTTY-ROOT; ADAM-AND-EVE (*Aplectrum hyemale*).

1. Flowering stem, x ½. 2. Mature capsules, x ½.
3. Habit of nonflowering plant, x ½. 4. Flower, x 1.
5. Capsule, x 1.

Sepals and petals purplish toward the base, brownish toward the tip; a single, plaited leaf produced in late summer remains green until flowering time the next spring. Moist, organic soils in woods. Occasionally seen in a few counties in southeastern Minnesota from Washington County southward.

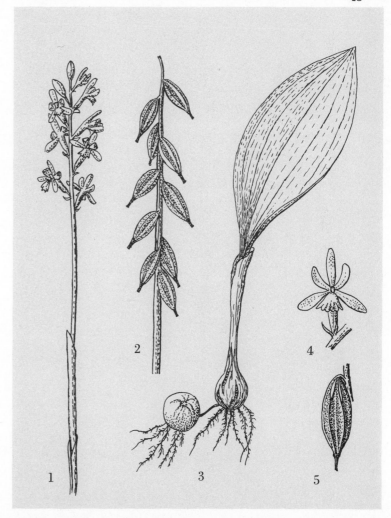

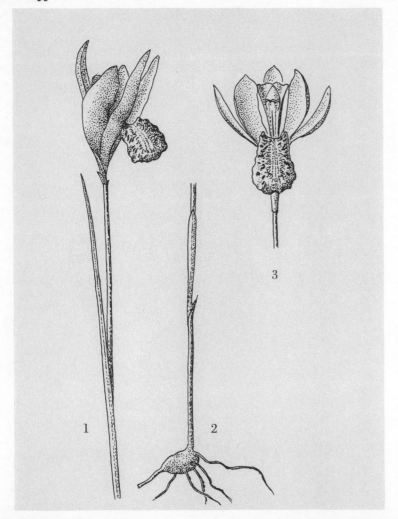

1

2

3

ORCHIDACEAE. *Orchid Family*

DRAGON'S MOUTH; SWAMP PINK (*Arethusa bulbosa*).

1–2. Habit of flowering stem, x 1. 3. Face view of flower, x 1.

Sepals and petals magenta-pink, the lip lighter pink, spotted and striped with purple and yellow. Sphagnum bogs and swampy meadows. Almost exclusively in the northeastern fifth of the state; seldom seen in abundance.

ORCHIDACEAE. *Orchid Family*

GRASS PINK; SWAMP PINK (*Calopogon pulchellus*).

1. Habit of flowering stem, x ¼. 2. Base of stem showing bulb, x 1. 3. Flower, x 1. 4. Capsule, x 1.

Sepals and petals rose-pink or lilac. Sphagnum bogs and swampy meadows. Central and eastern Minnesota.

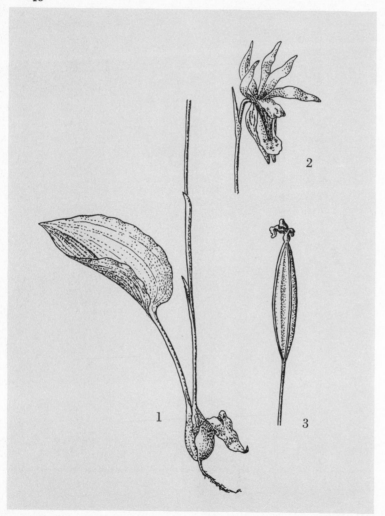

1 2 3

ORCHIDACEAE. *Orchid Family*

CALYPSO (*Calypso bulbosa*).

1–2. Habit of flowering plant, x 1. 3. Capsule, x 1.

Sepals and petals pale purple, the lip whitish, yellowish toward the tip, with brownish markings within, the apron white, spotted with purple and with 3 crests of yellow hairs. Moist coniferous forests. Northeastern quarter of the state; rare.

ORCHIDACEAE. *Orchid Family*

SPOTTED CORAL ROOT (*Corallorhiza maculata*).

1–2. Habit of flowering stem, x ½. 3. Stem with ripened capsules, x ½. 4. Flower, x 1.
5. Capsule, x 1.

Sepals and petals whitish, spotted or tinged with purple; stems pinkish-yellow to purplish or brown and lacking any green coloration. Dry woods. Common in the Arrowhead region of northeastern Minnesota; rare in the north-central and southeastern parts of the state. Three additional species of coral root are found in Minnesota.

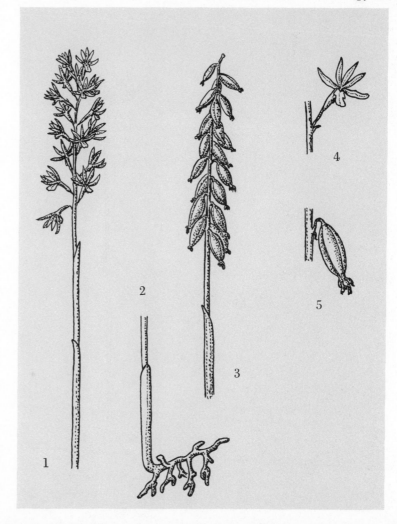

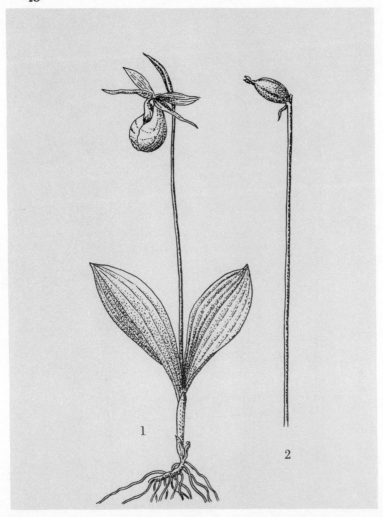

1

2

ORCHIDACEAE. *Orchid Family*

STEMLESS LADY-SLIPPER; MOCCASIN-FLOWER
(*Cypripedium acaule*).

1. Habit, x ⅓. 2. Capsule, x ⅓.

Sepals and lateral petals yellowish-green to greenish-brown, the lip pink, with red veins. Acid soil of bogs or seasonally wet coniferous woods. Central to north-central and northeastern Minnesota. Four additional species of lady-slipper orchids are found in the state.

ORCHIDACEAE. *Orchid Family*

YELLOW LADY-SLIPPER (*Cypripedium calceolus*).

1. Flowering stem, x ⅓. 2. Stem with mature capsule, x ⅓.

Sepals and lateral petals greenish-yellow to purplish-brown, the lip yellow, usually veined or spotted with purple. Occurring in a broad band from southeastern to northwestern Minnesota; rare in the Arrowhead counties. There are 2 distinguishable varieties in our flora which differ somewhat in flower size and habitat: var. *parviflorum*, the small yellow lady-slipper, is found in bogs, swamps, and along lakes; var. *pubescens*, the large yellow lady-slipper, is found in moist, upland woods.

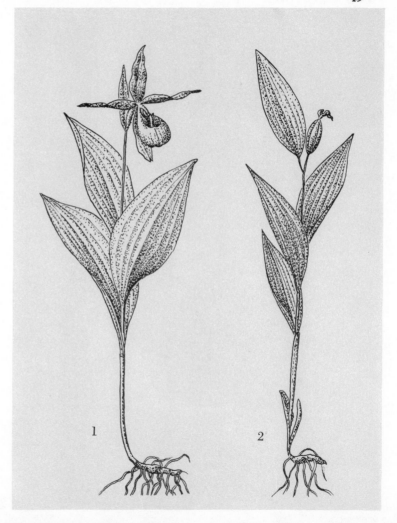

1   2   3

ORCHIDACEAE. *Orchid Family*

SHOWY LADY-SLIPPER (*Cypripedium reginae*).

1–2. Habit of flowering stem, x ⅓. 3. Stem with mature capsule, x ⅓.

Sepals and lateral petals white; lip white or suffused with pink and streaked with rose or purple. Openings in swamps, bogs, and very wet woods. Southeastern to north-central and northwestern Minnesota, east to St. Louis County. The official state flower.

ORCHIDACEAE. *Orchid Family*

DWARF RATTLESNAKE-PLANTAIN (*Goodyera repens*).
1–2. Habit of flowering stem, x 1. 3. Raceme with mature capsules, x 1. 4. Flower, x 4. 5. Leaf, x 1½.

Flowers white or greenish; leaves reticulate with white lines. Dry, coniferous, or mixed woods. North-central to northern Minnnesota; rare elsewhere. At least 2 more kinds of rattlesnake-plantain occur in the state.

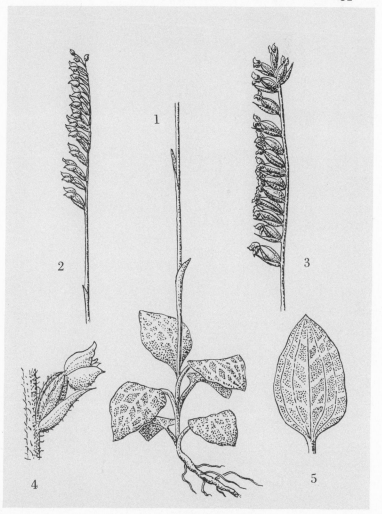

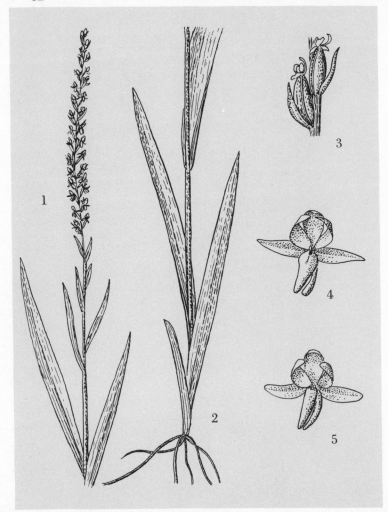

ORCHIDACEAE. *Orchid Family*

TALL WHITE ORCHID (*Habenaria dilatata*).

1–2. Habit of flowering plant, x ¼. 3. Nearly mature capsules, x 1. 4. Flower in face view, x 2.

Flowers white, strongly fragrant. Bogs, wet meadows, and woods. East-central, north-central, and north-eastern parts of the state.

NORTHERN OR LEAFY NORTHERN GREEN ORCHID (*Habenaria hyperborea*).

5. Flower in face view, x 2.

Flowers greenish or greenish-yellow. Habitat as above. Widely distributed in the state, but rare in the western and southern parts.

ORCHIDACEAE. *Orchid Family*

HOOKER'S ORCHID (*Habenaria hookeri*).

1. Habit, x ⅓. 2. Flower, x 1.

Flowers greenish or greenish-yellow, not stalked. Moist to dry woods. In counties bordering the Mississippi River in the southeastern section; also in north-central and northeastern Minnesota.

ROUND-LEAVED ORCHID (*Habenaria orbiculata*).

3. Habit, x ⅓. 4. Flower, x 1.

Very similar to the preceding. Flowers greenish-white, distinctly stalked, with a longer lip and spur. Moist to dry woods. North-central and northeastern Minnesota.

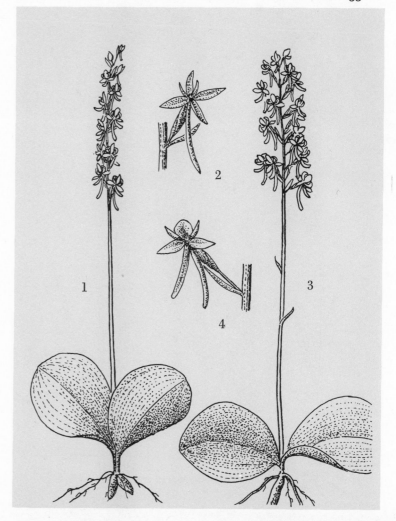

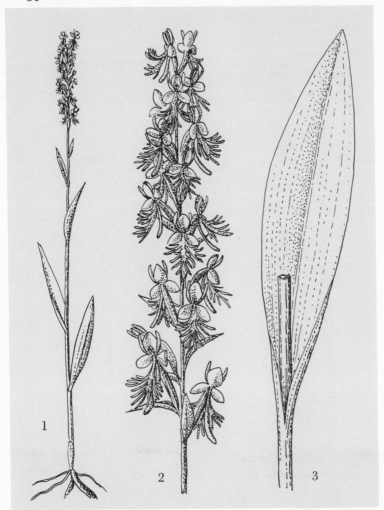

1   2   3

ORCHIDACEAE. *Orchid Family*

RAGGED-FRINGED ORCHID (*Habenaria lacera*).

1. Habit, x ¼. 2. Inflorescence, x 1. 3. Lowermost stem leaf, x 1.

Flowers yellowish-green or whitish. Open, wet meadows and swamps. East-central Minnesota, northward to St. Louis County.

ORCHIDACEAE. *Orchid Family*

PRAIRIE WHITE-FRINGED ORCHID (*Habenaria leucophaea*).

1. Inflorescence, x 1. 2. Lower stem leaf, x 1.

Flowers greenish-white or creamy-white. Wet meadows, prairies, and open swamps. Rare, in a broad band extending from Houston County in the southeast to Polk County in the northwest.

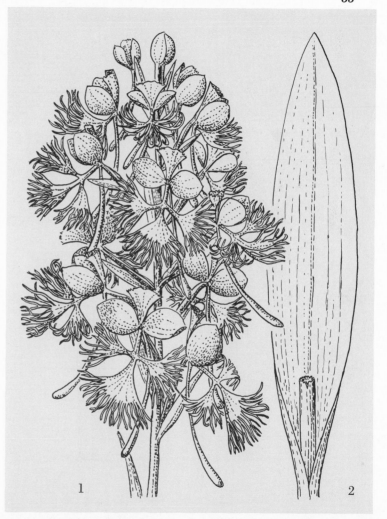

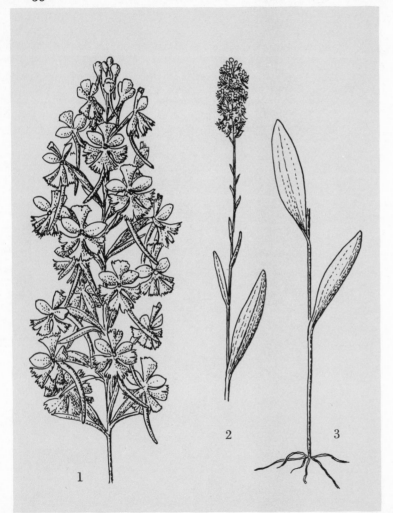

1

2

3

ORCHIDACEAE. *Orchid Family*

SMALL PURPLE-FRINGED ORCHID (*Habenaria psycodes*).

1. Inflorescence, x 1. 2–3. Habit, x ¼.

Flowers rose-purple or, rarely, white. Wet meadows and low, open woods. East-central to northeastern Minnesota; rare in the southeastern corner of the state.

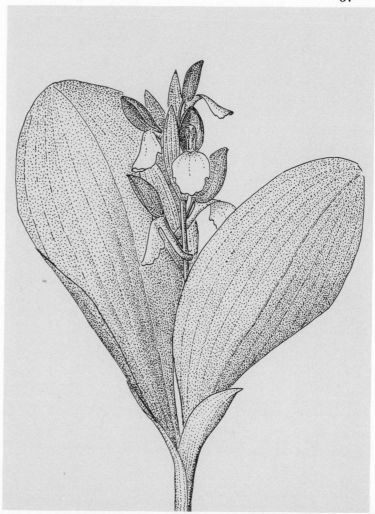

ORCHIDACEAE. *Orchid Family*

SHOWY ORCHIS (*Orchis spectabilis*).

Habit less underground parts, x 1.

Sepals and lateral petals pink to pale purple; lip white. Rich, mostly calcareous woods. Southeastern Minnesota, from Pope to Chisago counties in the north to Houston County in the southeast.

58

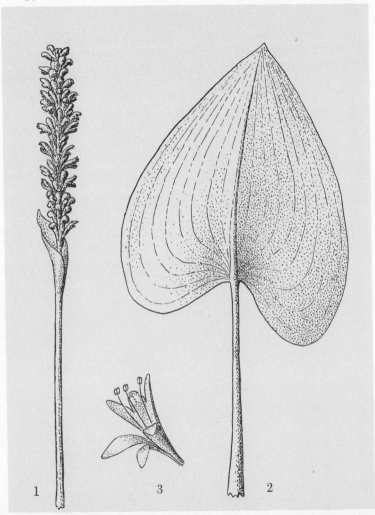

1   3   2

PONTEDERIACEAE. Pickerelweed Family

PICKERELWEED (*Pontederia cordata*).

1. Flowering stalk, x ½. 2. Leaf, x ½. 3. Flower, x 2.

Flowers violet-blue varying to white; flowering stems having a single large leaf and a foliar bract just beneath the spike of flowers; plants reproducing vegetatively by means of thick, fleshy rhizomes. Shallow water and muddy shores. Eastern side of Minnesota, from Wabasha County in the south to the Canadian border in St. Louis County in the north; central Minnesota west to Stearns County.

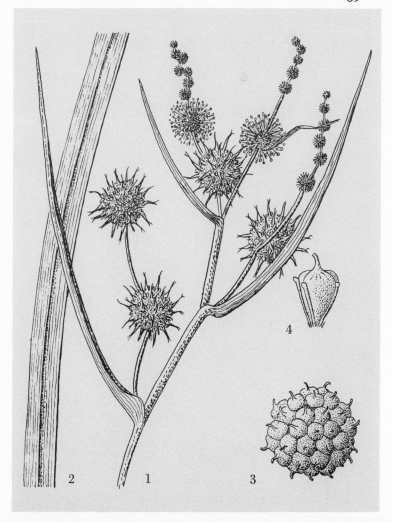

SPARGANIACEAE. Bur-Reed Family

BUR-REED (*Sparganium eurycarpum*).

1. Inflorescence and associated bracts, x 1. 2. Section of leaf, x 1. 3. Cluster of fruits, x 1. 4. Mature ovary and associated perianth, x 2.

Flowering heads greenish; stigmas 2; stems often 4 ft. or more tall; leaves stiff, pointed upward; plants spreading by means of buried rootstalks and forming colonies. In shallow water, edges of streams and lakes. Throughout the state. Eight species of bur-reed occur in the state. All grow in water and most have floating, ribbonlike leaves. Only this one has 2 stigmas.

1

3

2

SPARGANIACEAE. *Bur-Reed Family*

BUR-REED (*Sparganium fluctuans*).

1. Upper part of flowering stem and associated leaves, x 1. 2. Cluster of fruits, x 1. 3. Mature ovaries, x 3.

Flowering heads greenish; stigma 1; stems under water except for the flowering stalks; leaves ribbon-like and floating except for the bracteate floral ones; each fruit with a stout, curved beak; spreading by means of rootstocks. Quiet, shallow water of lakes and ponds. Distributed in the northeastern quarter of the state east of a line joining Kanabec, southern Clearwater, and northeastern Koochiching counties.

TYPHACEAE. Cattail Family

COMMON OR BROAD-LEAVED CATTAIL (*Typha latifolia*).

1. Upper part of plant in fruit, x ¼. 2. Upper part of plant in flower, x ½.

Mature pistillate spikes usually brown, mottled with darker brown; plants to 6 ft. or more tall. Shallow waters around lakes, marshes, and drainage ditches. Throughout the state.

NARROW-LEAVED CATTAIL (*Typha angustifolia*).

3. Upper part of plant in fruit, x ¼. 4. Upper part of plant in flower, x ½.

Mature pistillate spikes usually reddish-brown; plants to 5 ft. or more tall. Habitat as above, but not found in acidic waters. Throughout the state except in the northeastern quarter where it is absent except for local occurrences in southern St. Louis County and the fringes of adjacent counties.

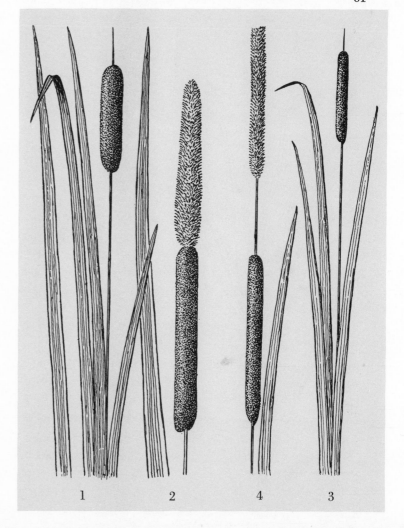

1   2   4   3

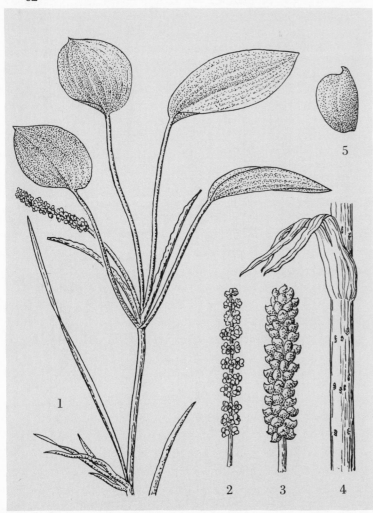

ZOSTERACEAE. *Pondweed Family*

FLOATING-LEAF PONDWEED (*Potamogeton natans*).

1. Upper part of stem, x ½. 2. Flowering spike, x 1.
3. Fruiting spike, x 1. 4. Section of old stem, x 3.
5. Achene, x 4.

Floating leaves rounded or notched at the base, leathery; underwater leaves long and narrow, with parallel margins. This perhaps is our most common species of floating-leaved pondweed; found in lakes and ponds throughout the central and northeastern parts of the state. The potamogetons constitute a group of over 25 species within the boundaries of the state.

ZOSTERACEAE. *Pondweed Family*

SAGO PONDWEED (*Potamogeton pectinatus*).

1. Upper portion of stem, x 1. 2. Section of stem with associated parts, x 2. 3. Part of fruiting spike, x 1. 4. Tip of leaf, x 4. 5. Achene, x 4.

Entire plant immersed except for the flowering spikes, stiff when removed from the water, the outer leaves on the branches pointed. Lakes and ponds throughout the state except in Cook and Lake counties.

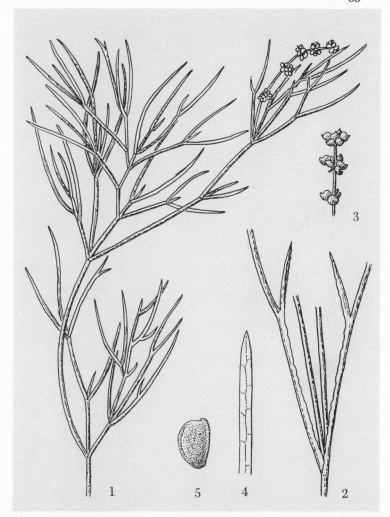

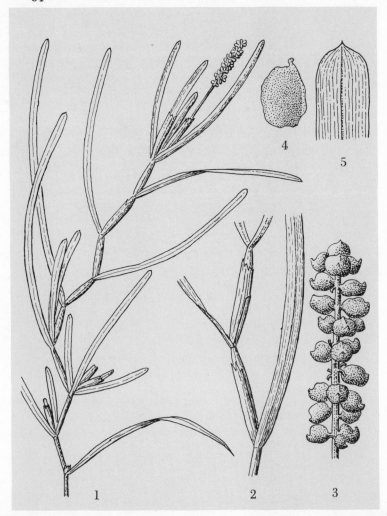

4

5

1

2

3

ZOSTERACEAE. *Pondweed Family*

FLATSTEM PONDWEED (*Potamogeton zosteriformis*).

1. Upper portion of stem, x ½. 2. Section of stem with associated parts, x 1. 3. Fruiting spike, x 2. 4. Achene, x 4. 5. Tip of leaf, x 4.

Entire plant immersed except for the flowering spikes; stems very flat. Lakes and ponds. Common throughout the state.

Dicotyledonae

THIS group of flowering plants is commonly termed the dicotyledons or dicots for short. Its members usually have leaves with a prominent midrib or central vein which gives rise to lesser veins along its length. Usually there are 4 or 5 flower parts of each kind in a single flower, that is, 4 or 5 sepals, petals, stamens, and carpels or, in some instances, the parts occur in multiples of 4 or 5. The embryonic plant within the seed normally has 2 seed leaves or cotyledons. Other equally important features of this group are found in the internal structure of the stem.

APOCYNACEAE. *Dogbane Family*

SPREADING DOGBANE (*Apocynum androsaemifolium*).

1. Upper part of stem, x 1. 2. Flower, x 2. 3. Interior of corolla, x 2. 4. Mature seed pods releasing seeds, x 1.

Corolla pink with red lines inside; juice milky. In partial shade at the edges of woods or in open sun. Found throughout most of the state.

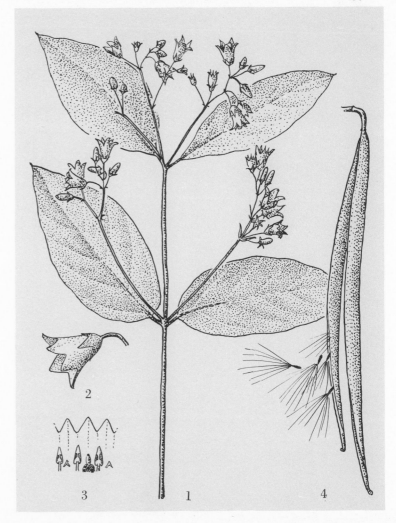

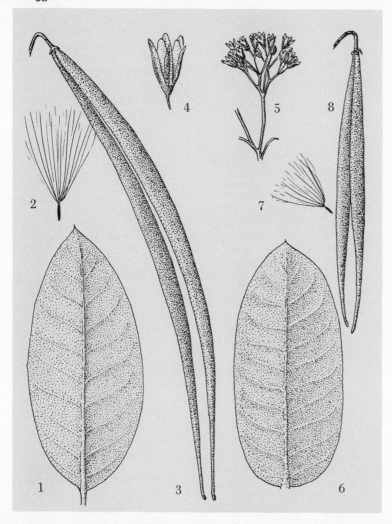

APOCYNACEAE. *Dogbane Family*

INDIAN HEMP (*Apocynum cannabinum*).

1. Leaf, x 1. 2. Seed, x 1. 3. Seed pods, x 1.
4. Flower, x 4. 5. Part of inflorescence, x 1.

Corolla whitish. Wet, open pastures and prairies. Southern and western parts of Minnesota.

INDIAN HEMP (*Apocynum sibiricum*).

6. Leaf, x 1. 7. Seed, x 1. 8. Seed pods, x 1.

Similar in appearance, but the leaves tend to be notched at the base. Western Minnesota.

ARALIACEAE. *Ginseng Family*

BRISTLY SARSAPARILLA (*Aralia hispida*).

1. Stem, x ⅕. 2. Leaf, x ½. 3. Flower, x 3.
4. Fruit, x 3.

Flowers white or greenish. Rocky and sandy shores and open woods. Mainly in the Arrowhead counties south to Pine County and westward to Upper Red Lake and the Northwest Angle.

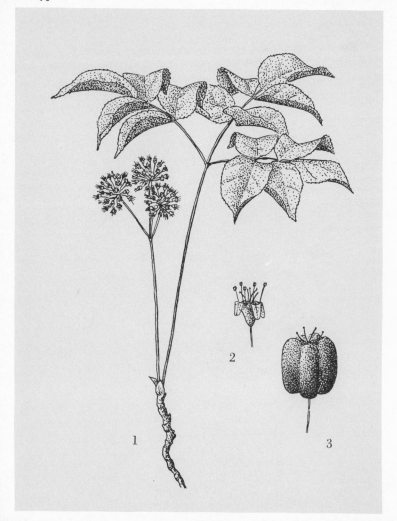

ARALIACEAE. *Ginseng Family*

WILD SARSAPARILLA (*Aralia nudicaulis*).

1. Habit, x ¼. 2. Flower, x 3. 3. Fruit, x 3.

Flowers white or greenish; flowering stalks produced from the crown at ground level. Moist woods. Throughout the state, but rare in the prairie counties of the south and west.

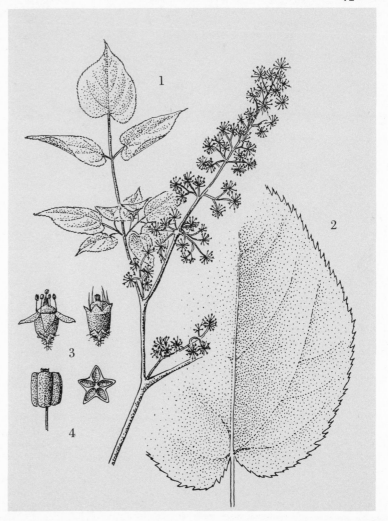

ARALIACEAE. *Ginseng Family*

SPIKENARD (*Aralia racemosa*).

1. End of branch showing compound leaf and inflorescence, x ¼. 2. A single leaflet, x 1. 3. Flowers, side view, the one to the right with petals and anthers removed, x 8. 4. Fruits, the first in side view, the second in transverse section, x 4.

Flowers white or greenish. Rich, moist woods. Throughout the state except in the prairie counties of the south and west.

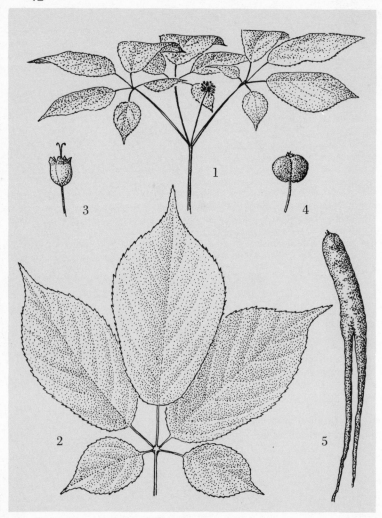

ARALIACEAE. *Ginseng Family*

GINSENG (*Panax quinquefolius*).

1. Top of stem showing inflorescence and leaves, x ¼.
2. A single compound leaf, x ½. 3. Flower with petals removed, x 4. 4. Fruit, x 1. 5. Root, x ½.

Flowers greenish-white; fruit bright red; flower stalk arising at the top of the stem; root often branched. Rich woods. Southeastern Minnesota, north to Mille Lacs County and west to Jackson County on the Iowa border. Now extremely rare.

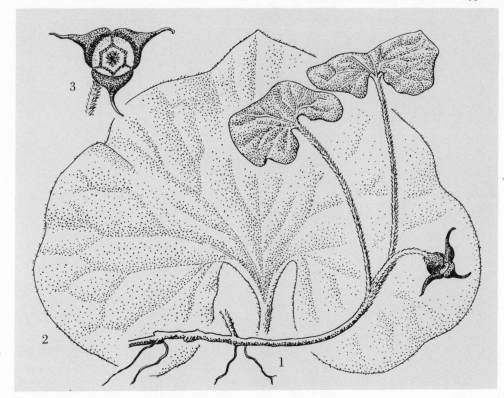

ARISTOLOCHIACEAE.
Birthwort Family

WILD GINGER (*Asarum canadense*).

1. Plant in early spring, x ½.
2. Leaf, x 1. 3. Face view of flower, x 1.

Flowers reddish-purple, appearing with the young leaves; plants reproducing by creeping rhizomes as well as by seeds; forming colonies. Rich woods. Eastern half of the state; more infrequent westward to Becker and Redwood counties.

74

ASCLEPIADACEAE. *Milkweed Family*

SWAMP MILKWEED (*Asclepias incarnata*).

1. Upper part of stem, x ¾. 2. Leaf, x ¾. 3. Seed pod and seed, x ¾.

Flowers pink to rose-purple. Open swamps and wet prairies. Throughout the state.

ASCLEPIADACEAE. Milkweed Family

SHOWY MILKWEED (*Asclepias speciosa*).

1. Upper part of stem, x ¾. 2. Flower in side view, x 1. 3. Seed pod, x ¾.

Flowers greenish-purple. Prairies. Almost exclusively confined to the prairie areas of the western third of the state.

1

2

ASCLEPIADACEAE. *Milkweed Family*

COMMON MILKWEED (*Asclepias syriaca*).

1. Upper part of stem, x ⅓. 2. Flower in side view, x 1.

Flowers purple to greenish, fragrant; plants spreading vigorously by means of creeping, subterranean rhizomes as well as by seeds. Meadows, fields, roadsides, and waste areas, in full sun. Throughout the state, but rare in the northern and northeastern sections.

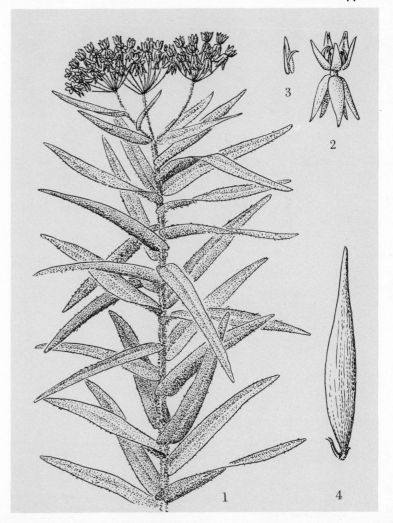

ASCLEPIADACEAE. *Milkweed Family*

BUTTERFLY-WEED (*Asclepias tuberosa*).

1. Upper part of stem, x ½. 2. Flower in side view, x 2. 3. One of 5 divisions of the corona present in the flower showing the horn, x 2. 4. Seed pod, x ½.

Flowers bright yellow to greenish-orange or red; annual stems produced from a branched crown; root deep-set. Dry prairies or sunny, open woods, usually in sandy soil. East-central and southern Minnesota.

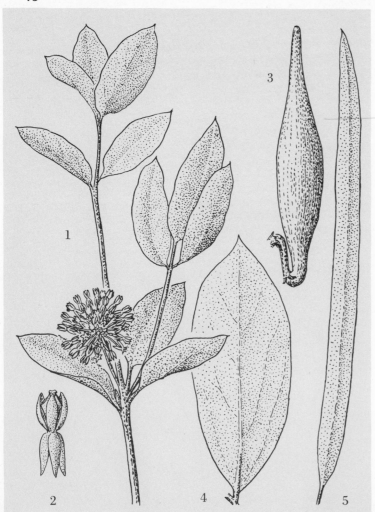

ASCLEPIADACEAE. *Milkweed Family*

GREEN MILKWEED (*Asclepias viridiflora*).

1. Upper part of stem, x ½. 2. Flower in side view, x 2. 3. Seed pod, x 1. 4–5. Leaves showing the extreme variations found on different plants, x 1.

Flowers greenish-yellow; root deep-set. Open woods and prairies, especially in sandy soil. Central, southern, and western Minnesota, north to Mille Lacs and Polk counties.

BALSAMINACEAE. *Jewelweed Family*

SPOTTED TOUCH-ME-NOT; JEWELWEED (*Impatiens capensis*).

1. Upper part of stem, x 1. 2. Flower in face view, x 1.

Corolla orange-yellow spotted with reddish-brown, rarely lemon-yellow or white; seed pods opening explosively; stems succulent. Wet or springy places, in partial or full shade. Throughout the state; uncommon in prairie areas of the west and south.

PALE TOUCH-ME-NOT; JEWELWEED (*Impatiens pallida*).

3. Flower in side view, x 1.

Corolla pale yellow spotted with reddish-brown, sometimes unspotted or creamy-yellow; seed pods and stems as above. Habitat as above. In a diagonal band, Houston to Big Stone counties; absent from the northern two-thirds of the state and from the southern and southwestern border areas.

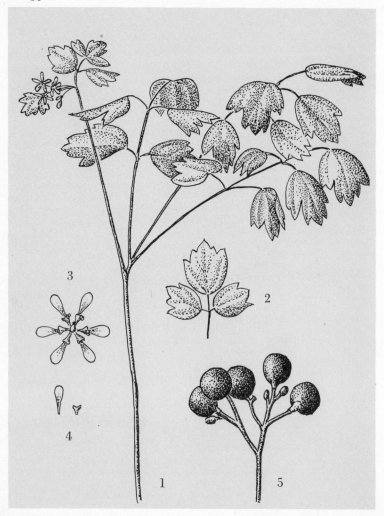

BERBERIDACEAE. *Barberry Family*

BLUE COHOSH (*Caulophyllum thalictroides*).

1. Upper part of stem, x ¼. 2. Small portion of the compound leaf with 3 leaflets shown, x ¼. 3. Flower in face view, x 2. 4. Sepal and petal, x 2. 5. Inflorescence in fruit, x 1.

Flowers yellowish-green or purplish, appearing with the young leaves; seeds stalked, spherical, green at first, turning blue, the outer coat fleshy. Moist, rich woods. Generally distributed; rare or absent in the northern and northeastern sections; absent in the prairie zone except in relict wooded sites.

BERBERIDACEAE. *Barberry Family*

MAY APPLE; MANDRAKE (*Podophyllum peltatum*).

1. Upper part of stem, x ¼. 2. Face view of flower, x ½. 3. Berry, x ½.

Flowers waxy-white, nodding; fruit a large, fleshy, ovoid, many seeded berry, greenish-white at first, turning yellow when ripe; berries edible, the seeds and herbage poisonous. Rich, open woods and adjacent pastures, usually in partial shade. Southeastern Minnesota north to Goodhue County and west to Freeborn and Rice counties.

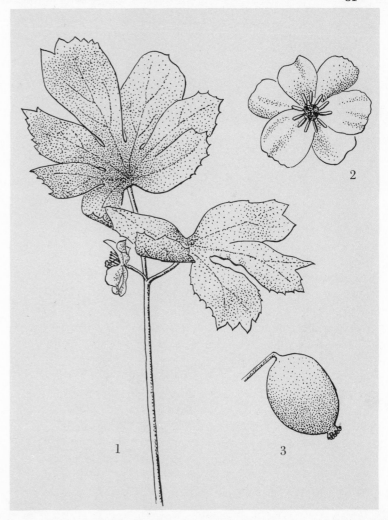

BORAGINACEAE. Borage Family

HOARY PUCCOON (*Lithospermum canescens*).

1. Habit, x ⅓. 2. Inflorescence, x 1. 3. Interior of corolla, x 1.

Corolla orange; stems and leaves grayish with a dense covering of soft hairs which lie close to the surface. Open, sandy woods and prairies. Throughout much of Minnesota, but rare or absent in several northeastern and northern counties.

HAIRY OR CAROLINA PUCCOON (*Lithospermum caroliniense*).

4. Upper part of stem, x 1. 5. Interior of corolla, x 1.

Corolla orange-yellow; stems and leaves rough, with stiff, spreading hairs. Dry prairies and open woods, especially in sandy soil. East-central Minnesota and in the southeast, in counties bordering the Mississippi River.

BORAGINACEAE. *Borage Family*

NARROW-LEAVED PUCCOON (*Lithospermum incisum*).

1. Habit, x ½. 2. Upper part of stem, x 1. 3. Interior of corolla, x 1. 4. Mature ovary with seeds included and a persistent calyx, x 1.

Corolla lemon-yellow, the lobes fringed or toothed; surfaces of leaves covered with stiff, appressed hairs. Dry prairies. Southern and western Minnesota, south and west of a line joining Ramsey, Otter Tail, and Kittson counties.

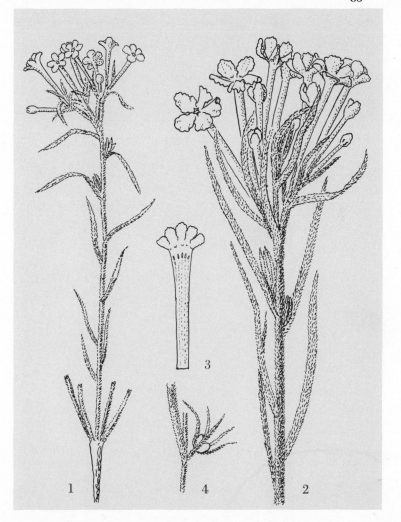

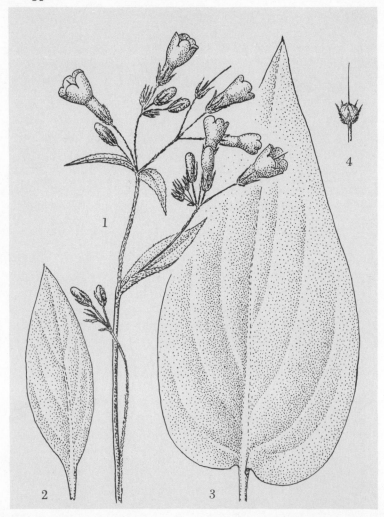

BORAGINACEAE. Borage Family

TALL LUNGWORT (*Mertensia paniculata*).

1. Upper part of stem, x 1. 2. Stem leaf, x 1.
3. Basal leaf, x 1. 4. Mature ovary, x 1.

Corolla blue, pink when in bud; leaves and stems
hairy, and rough. Damp thickets and woods. In the
northeastern quarter of the state, north and east of
a line connecting Carlton, Clearwater, and Lake of
the Woods counties; also reported from Fillmore
County.

BORAGINACEAE. *Borage Family*

BLUEBELL; VIRGINIA COWSLIP (*Mertensia virginica*).

1. Upper part of stem, x 1. 2. Root, x ½.
3. Basal leaf, x ½.

Corolla blue, pink when in bud; surfaces of leaves and stems completely smooth, bluish; plants drying up and disappearing after the seeds are dropped. Rich woods and bottom lands. In the southeastern corner of the state, north to Wabasha and west to Blue Earth counties.

1

2

3

BORAGINACEAE. *Borage Family*

FALSE GROMWELL (*Onosmodium molle*).

1. Upper part of stem, x ¾. 2. Side view of flower, x 1½. 3. Mature segment of ovary including the seed within and the persistent calyx, x 1½.

Corolla dull, greenish- or yellowish-white; stems and leaves covered throughout with spreading hairs, giving the plants a grayish appearance; annual stems several to many from a branched crown, often forming large clumps. Prairies. Southern and western Minnesota, south and west of a line joining Hennepin, Stearns, Mahnomen, and Kittson counties.

CACTACEAE. *Cactus Family*

PRICKLY PEAR; BRITTLE OPUNTIA
(*Opuntia fragilis*).

1. Habit, x ½. 2. Terminal joint with flower and bud, x 1.

Flowers yellow; jointed stems forming dense masses. Edges of boulders or rocky outcrops or in low, flat, eroded prairies. At scattered localities in Chisago, Scott, and Stearns counties; more common along the Minnesota River from Renville to Big Stone counties and in Pipestone and Rock counties. Another prickly pear, *O. humifusa*, having larger, flatter stem joints, is found in similar habitats in southwestern Minnesota, from Blue Earth to Yellow Medicine counties; also in Rock and Pipestone counties.

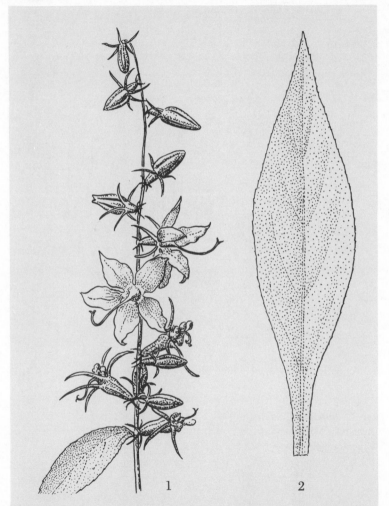

1   2

CAMPANULACEAE. *Bluebell Family*

TALL BELLFLOWER (*Campanula americana*).

1. Upper part of stem, x 1. 2. Lower stem leaf, x ¾.

Corolla blue; plants annual; stems 2–6 ft. tall. Moist woods and areas around springs, in full or partial sun. Found in a broad strip joining Houston County in the southeast and Hennepin, Brown, and Chippewa counties in the north and west.

CAMPANULACEAE. *Bluebell Family*

HAREBELL; BLUEBELL (*Campanula rotundifolia*).

1–2. Upper and middle sections of the stem, x 1.
3. Mature capsule, x 2.

Corolla blue, purplish-blue or fading toward white; stems from a branched, perennial crown, often forming dense clumps, a few inches to a foot or more tall; basal leaves about as broad as long, pointed at the tip and toothed at the edge. Dry meadows, open woods, rocky shores, usually in sandy soils. Generally distributed in the state except in the border counties along the south and in the southwestern counties.

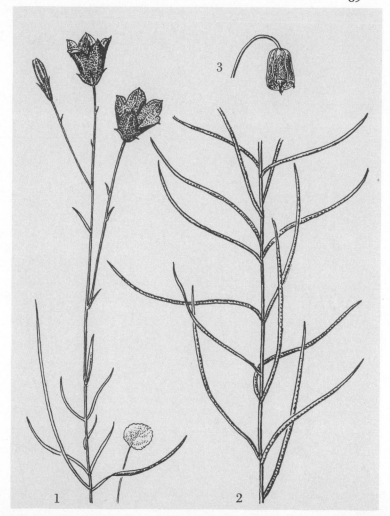

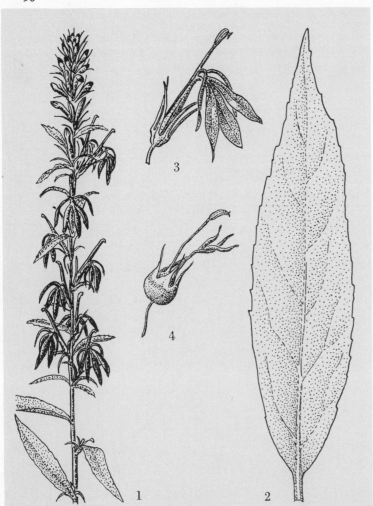

1

3

4

2

CAMPANULACEAE. *Bluebell Family*

CARDINAL-FLOWER (*Lobelia cardinalis*).

1. Upper part of stem, x ½. 2. Leaf, x 1. 3. Side view of flower, x 1. 4. Nearly mature capsule with sepals and remnants of corolla, x 1.

Corolla scarlet; stems 1–3 ft. or more tall. Wet soil, shores, and meadows. In counties bordering the Mississippi River from Washington to Houston counties.

CAMPANULACEAE. *Bluebell Family*

GREAT LOBELIA; BLUE CARDINAL-FLOWER (*Lobelia siphilitica*).

1–2. Upper and middle sections of stem, x 1.
3. Calyx, x 2.

Corolla usually blue, rarely white; stems 1–3 ft. or more tall. Low, sunny woods, swamps, and wet ground. Southeastern, central, and western Minnesota.

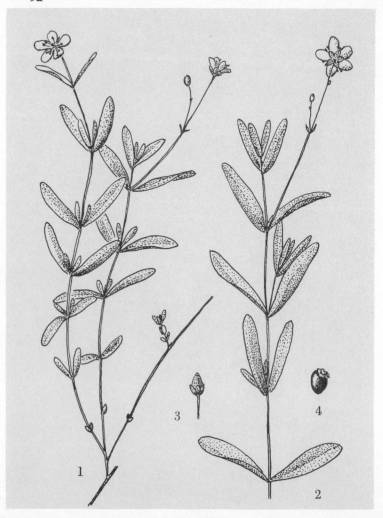

1

2

3

4

CARYOPHYLLACEAE. *Pink Family*

SANDWORT (*Arenaria lateriflora*).

1–2. Upper parts of stem, x 1. 3. Capsule, x 1.
4. Seed, x 5.

Corolla white. Woods, sometimes in open grassy areas. Found in most parts of the state; evidently absent in the southwestern corner.

CARYOPHYLLACEAE. *Pink Family*

FIELD CHICKWEED (*Cerastium arvense*).

1. Habit, x 1. 2. Face and rear views of flower, x 1.
3. Opened capsule, x 1.

Corolla white; stems matted at the base. Fields and
pastures, sometimes a weed; often in sandy places.
Occurs most commonly in the western half of the
state; occasionally seen elsewhere.

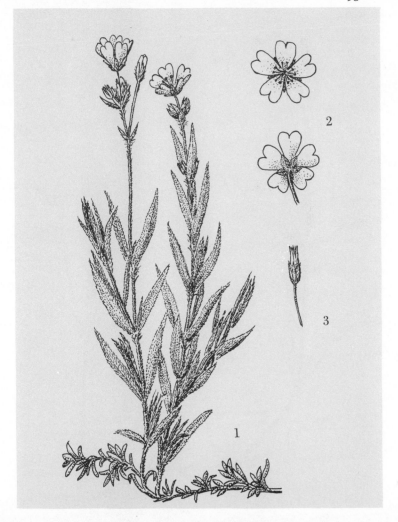

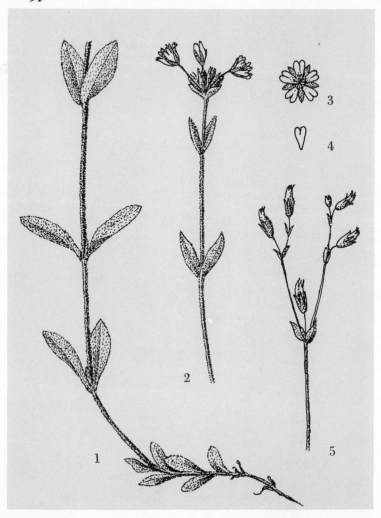

CARYOPHYLLACEAE. *Pink Family*

COMMON MOUSE-EAR CHICKWEED (*Cerastium vulgatum*).

1–2. Lower and upper sections of stem, x 1. 3. Face view of flower, x 1. 4. Petal, x 1. 5. Inflorescence with mature capsules, x 1.

Corolla white; stems and leaves covered with hair, viscid (sticky); stems frequently reclining and matted at the base. Most commonly seen in the eastern half of the state; rare westward.

CARYOPHYLLACEAE. *Pink Family*

WHITE CAMPION (*Lychnis alba*).

1. Upper part of stem, x ¼. 2. Joint of stem showing paired leaves, x 1. 3. Face and side view of petal, x 1. 4–5. Face and side view of male flower, x 1. 6. Female flower and mature capsule enclosed by calyx, x 1.

Corolla white; flowers fragrant, unisexual, the male and female flowers on separate plants. Disturbed soil in pastures and abandoned fields and along roadways; introduced from Europe and now a common weed. Generally distributed throughout the state.

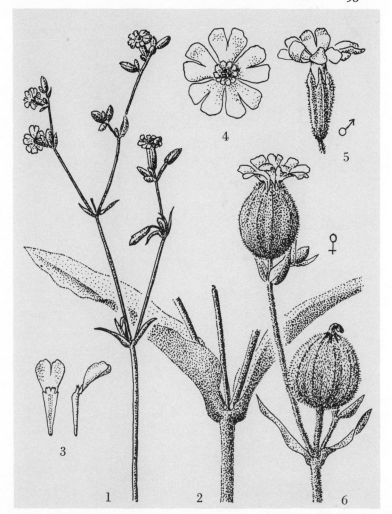

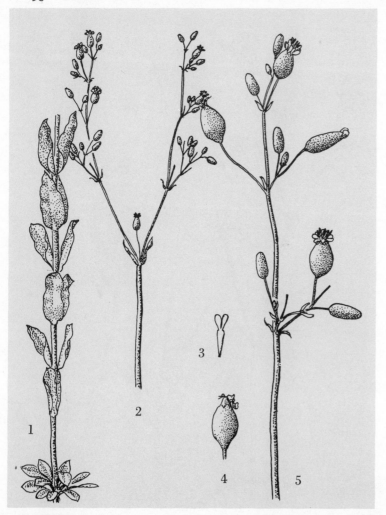

1

2

3

4

5

CARYOPHYLLACEAE. *Pink Family*

SMOOTH CATCHFLY (*Silene cserei*).

1–2. Lower and upper sections of stem, x ¼. 3. Petal, x 1. 4. Mature capsule enclosed in calyx, x 1. 5. Branch of inflorescence, x 1.

Corolla white or pinkish; stems and leaves smooth, bluish. Roadsides and waste places; introduced from Europe. Generally distributed around the state, but apparently absent in the southwestern parts.

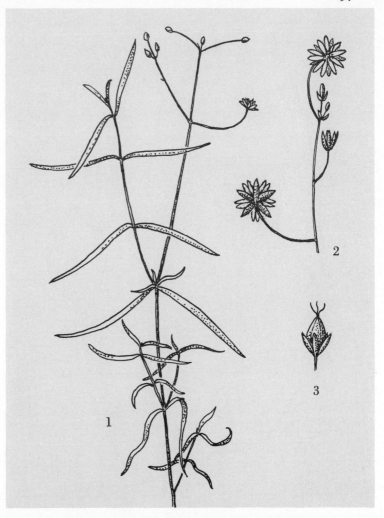

CARYOPHYLLACEAE. *Pink Family*

LONG-LEAVED CHICKWEED (*Stellaria longifolia*).

1. Upper part of stem, x 1. 2. Branch of inflorescence showing 5 sepals and 5 deeply forked petals in each flower, x 2. 3. Capsule, x 2.

Corolla white; stems weak, often reclining. Moist places, usually in woods. Throughout the state, but commonest in the wooded sections.

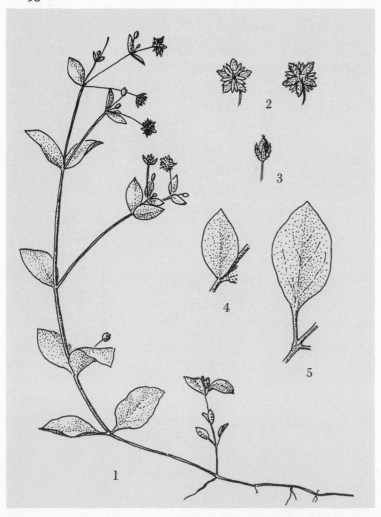

CARYOPHYLLACEAE. *Pink Family*

COMMON CHICKWEED (*Stellaria media*).

1. Habit, x ½. 2. Face and rear view of flower, x 1.
3. Capsule, x 1. 4. Leaf at upper joint of stem, x 1.
5. Leaf at lower joint of stem, x 1.

Corolla white; stems trailing at the base. Moist, low areas in lawns, borders, and fields, mostly in full sun; introduced from Europe. Found throughout the state, often a noxious weed.

COMPOSITAE. *Composite Family*

YARROW; MILFOIL (*Achillea millefolium*).

1. Upper half of stem (European form), x ¾.
2. Flowering head, x 2. 3. Upper half of stem
(American form), x ¾.

Ray flowers white or more rarely pink or purple;
plants aromatic; reproduces by underground stems
as well as by seeds; introduced and native. The
European form has greener foliage and the cluster
of heads has a flatter top; the native, more common
form appears ashy-gray in color from the denser
cover of hairs on the stems and leaves. Moist to dry
habitats, usually in full sun, the introduced form
usually in disturbed soil around farms. Throughout
the state.

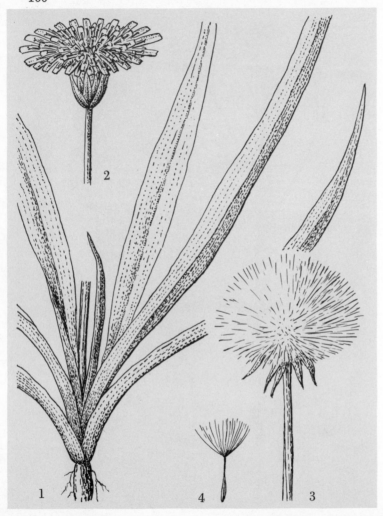

COMPOSITAE. *Composite Family*

AGOSERIS; FALSE DANDELION (*Agoseris glauca*).

1. Base of plant, x 1. 2. Flowering head, x 1.
3. Fruiting head, x 1. 4. Achene, x 1.

Ray flowers yellow, sometimes tinged with pink or purple; leaves smooth, nearly or entirely without hair, bluish. Prairies and meadows. Rock to Kittson and Roseau counties. Another kind of false dandelion, *A. cuspidata*, is found at scattered localities in southern and southwestern Minnesota, south and west of a line connecting Washington and Clay counties. It is very similar in appearance, but differs in having the leaves woolly along the edges and in several small features of the achenes.

COMPOSITAE. *Composite Family*

PEARLY EVERLASTING (*Anaphalis margaritacea*).

1. Upper part of stem, x 1. 2. Flowering heads, x 2.

Bracts of flowering heads pearly-white; plants covered with white wool; spreading by means of underground stems. Moist to dry habitats, in open sun to partial shade. Central, eastern, and north-eastern Minnesota north of Goodhue County and east of Becker County.

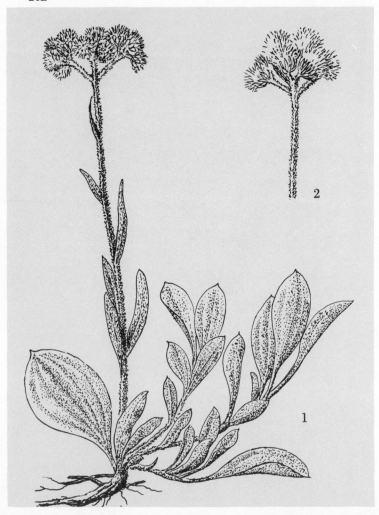

2

1

COMPOSITAE. *Composite Family*

EVERLASTING; PUSSY-TOES; LADIES TOBACCO
(*Antennaria plantaginifolia*).

1. Habit of staminate plant, x 1. 2. Inflorescence of pistillate plant, x 1.

Bracts of flowering heads white or purplish; corollas and styles often red; plants of 2 kinds, staminate (producing the pollen) or pistillate (producing the seeds), both kinds reproducing vigorously by stolons and forming colonies. The 2 kinds have quite distinct appearances at flowering time. Open, dry woods, fields, and prairies. Found in a diagonal band from Houston County to Kittson County. One or another of the several species of everlasting is found in all parts of the state.

COMPOSITAE. *Composite Family*

DOGFENNEL; CHAMOMILE (*Anthemis cotula*).

1. Upper part of stem, x 1. 2. Compound leaf, x 1.

Ray flowers white; stems 0.5–1.5 ft. tall; herbage strongly scented; plants annual. Old fields, roadsides, and waste places; introduced from Europe, now a cosmopolitan weed. Found in southern Minnesota south of a line connecting Washington and Chippewa counties; scattered records in Clay, Itasca, Carlton, and St. Louis counties.

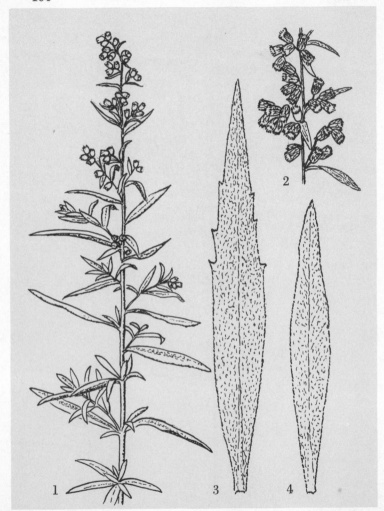

1

2

3

4

COMPOSITAE. *Composite Family*

WESTERN MUGWORT; WHITE SAGE (*Artemisia ludoviciana*).

1. Upper part of stem, x ½. 2. Inflorescence, x 1. 3–4. Lower and upper stem leaves, x 1.

Flowering heads greenish or grayish; leaves and stems densely covered with white hair; reproducing and spreading rapidly by means of underground stems. Prairies and pastures. In southern and western Minnesota. Altogether, we have about 12 kinds of *Artemisia* within the state. Those with woody stems are often called wormwoods.

COMPOSITAE. *Composite Family*

LINDLEY'S ASTER (*Aster ciliolatus*).

1. Upper part of stem, x ½. 2. Flowering head, x 2.
3. Lower stem leaf, x ½.

Ray flowers blue. Dry, open woods and thickets.
Common in the northern and northeastern two-thirds
of the state; rare or absent from the southern and
southwestern third. About 25 species of wild asters
are native to Minnesota.

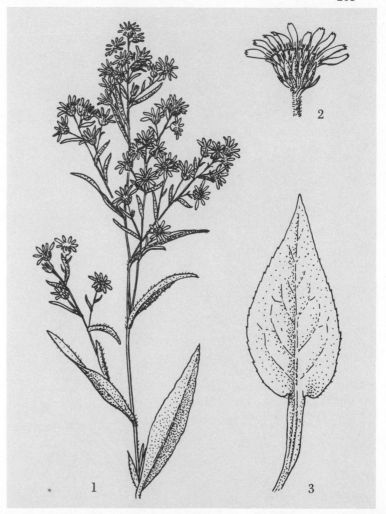

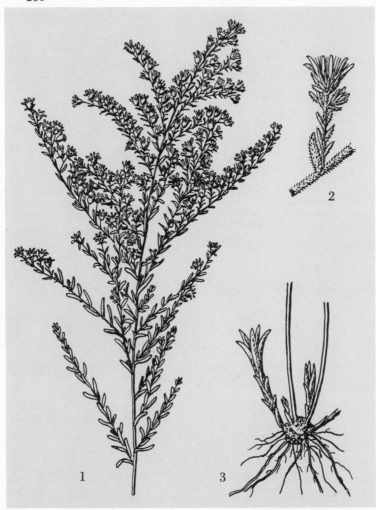

1

2

3

COMPOSITAE. Composite Family

FROST-WEED ASTER (*Aster ericoides*).

1. Upper part of stem, x ½. 2. Short branch with flowering head, x 2. 3. Base of plant, x ½.

Ray flowers white or occasionally light blue or pink; spreading vigorously by underground stems. Dry, open places, especially in the prairie. Common in the southern and western two-thirds of the state; rare in the northeastern section.

COMPOSITAE. *Composite Family*

SMOOTH ASTER (*Aster laevis*).

1–2. Habit, x ½. 3. Flowering head, x 2. 4–5. Lower and upper stem leaves, x ½.

Ray flowers blue or purple; stem and leaf surfaces smooth, bluish. Dry, open places in fields and woods. Over most of the state, but rare in the Arrowhead and adjacent counties.

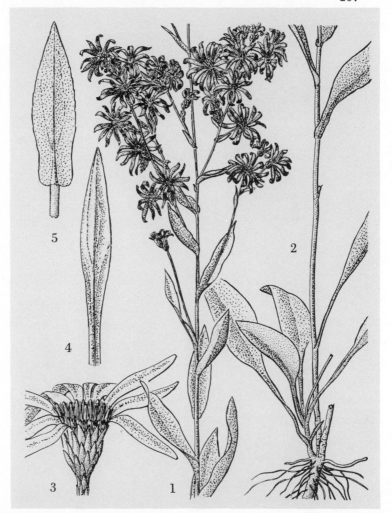

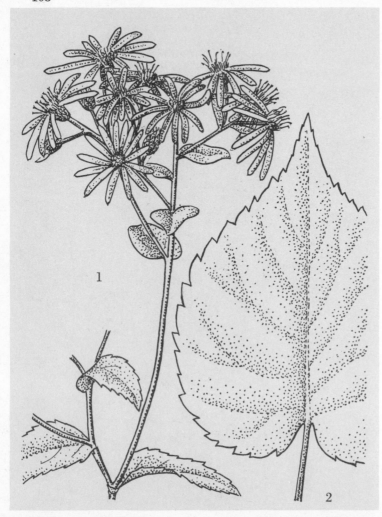

COMPOSITAE. Composite Family

LARGE-LEAVED ASTER (*Aster macrophyllus*).

1. Upper part of stem, x 1. 2. Basal leaf, x 1.

Ray flowers tinged with lilac or purple; stems with glandular hairs at the top; spreading vigorously from rootstocks and forming colonies. Moist or dry, open woods and forests. Central, east-central, and northeastern Minnesota.

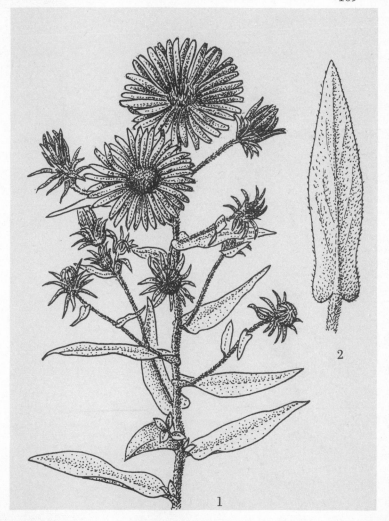

COMPOSITAE. *Composite Family*

NEW ENGLAND ASTER (*Aster novae-angliae*).

1. Upper part of stem, x 1. 2. Stem leaf, x 1.

Ray flowers reddish-purple, rose, violet, or white; stems clumped, usually 3 or 4 or even 6 ft. high, covered with hair. Moist to wet low places, in full sun. Southern and western Minnesota south and west of a line joining Goodhue, Stearns, and Roseau counties.

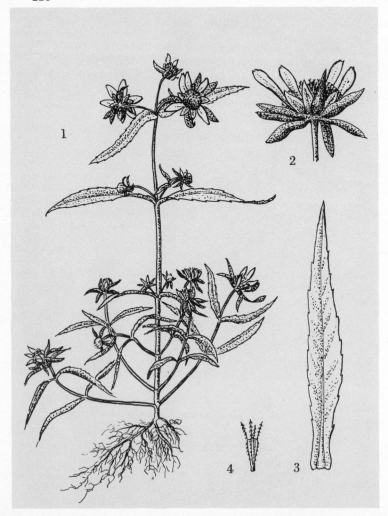

1

2

4   3

COMPOSITAE. *Composite Family*

STICK-TIGHT; BEGGAR-TICKS (*Bidens cernua*).

1. Habit, x ½. 2. Flowering head, x 1. 3. Stem leaf, x 1. 4. Achene, x 2.

Ray flowers yellow; flowering heads drooping or nodding as they grow older. Low, wet places, edges of ponds, lakes, and streams. Throughout the state. About 7 kinds of stick-tight occur in Minnesota; all are similar in appearance, but this one is probably the most representative.

COMPOSITAE. *Composite Family*

GREAT INDIAN PLANTAIN (*Cacalia muhlenbergii*).

1. Upper part of stem, x ¼. 2. Branch of inflorescence, x 1.

Flowers of the head whitish, all tubular; leaves without hair, green on both sides. Woods. Southeastern Minnesota east of a line connecting Goodhue and Mower counties.

TUBEROUS INDIAN PLANTAIN (*Cacalia tuberosa*).

3. Lower part of stem, x ¼.

Flowers and leaves as described above; the leaf form, as shown, is very different; root thickened. Wet prairies. Southeastern Minnesota, as far north and west as Scott, Nicollet, and Brown counties.

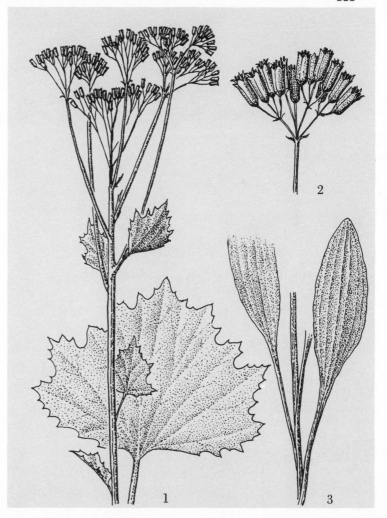

112

COMPOSITAE. Composite Family

CHICORY (*Cichorium intybus*).

1. Branch of stem, x 1. 2. Lower stem and basal leaves, x ¼.

Flowers bright blue, rarely pink or white. Waste fields and roadsides. Native of Eurasia, but fully naturalized in the United States. In Minnesota, found at a few scattered localities in the southern and northeastern parts of the state.

COMPOSITAE. *Composite Family*

OX-EYE DAISY (*Chrysanthemum leucanthemum*).

1–2. Top sections of stem showing opened and unopened flowering heads, x 1. 3. Basal leaf, x 1.

Ray flowers white; perennial from underground stems. Roadsides, fields, and waste places. Naturalized from Europe. Most commonly seen in the eastern half of the state.

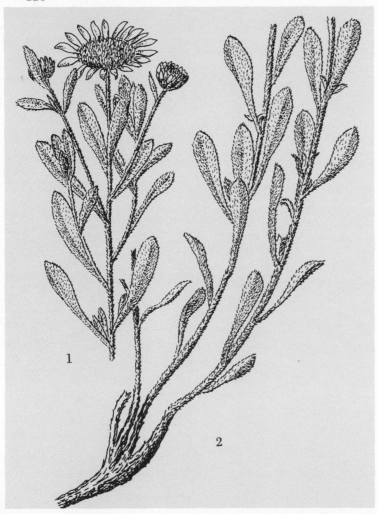

1

2

COMPOSITAE. *Composite Family*

GOLDEN ASTER (*Chrysopsis villosa*).

1–2. Habit of plant, x 1.

Ray flowers yellow; several spreading stems arising from a branched crown and deep taproot; foliage and stems covered with hair. Dry, often sandy soil, hills, and prairies, in full sun. East-central, southwestern and northwestern Minnesota; rare in the northeastern section.

COMPOSITAE. *Composite Family*

HILL'S THISTLE (*Cirsium hillii*).

1. Upper part of stem with flowering head, x 1.
2. Stem and basal leaves, x ½. 3. Innermost, middle, and outermost involucral bracts, x 1.

Flowers purple, rarely white; stems usually less than 18 in. tall; perennial from root sprouts. Low, rather moist meadows, usually sandy soil. Found in a narrow zone connecting Houston and Otter Tail counties. In addition to this one, there are 5 native and 2 introduced species of thistles in Minnesota.

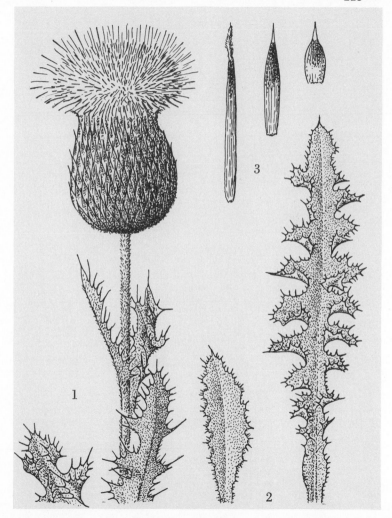

116

COMPOSITAE. *Composite Family*

SWAMP THISTLE (*Cirsium muticum*).

1. Upper part of stem with heads at various stages, x 1. 2. Basal leaf, x ½. 3. Outermost, middle, and innermost involucral bracts in graded series, x 2.

Flowers purple, rarely white; roots shallow, succulent; biennial. Sunny, wet meadows and swamps, organic soil. Generally distributed in the state except in the south and southwest.

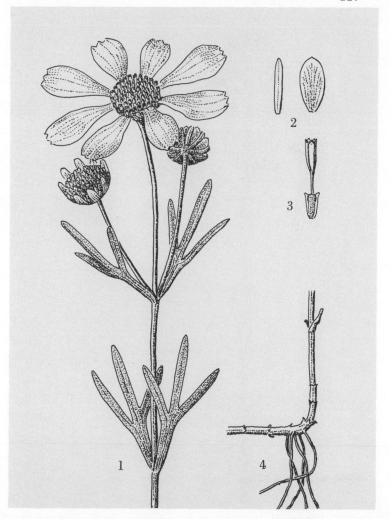

COMPOSITAE. *Composite Family*

TICKSEED (*Coreopsis palmata*).

1. Upper part of stem, x 1. 2. Outer and inner in-volucral bracts, x 2. 3. Disc flower, x 2. 4. Lower part of stem joined to rootstock, x 1.

Ray flowers yellow; perennial, spreading from root-stocks. Prairies and open woods. In the southern half of the state south of a line joining Chisago and Otter Tail counties.

118

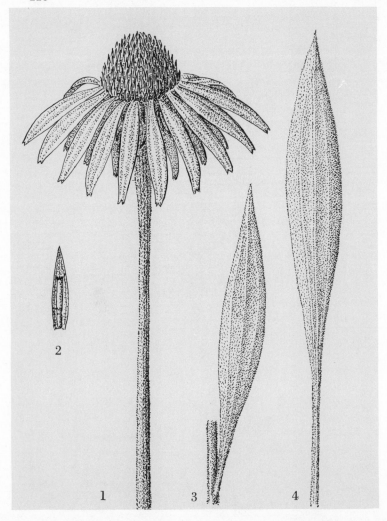

COMPOSITAE. *Composite Family*

CONEFLOWER; NARROW-LEAVED PURPLE CONE-FLOWER (*Echinacea angustifolia*).

1. Flowering head, x 1. 2. Involucral bract, x 2. 3. Stem leaf, x 1. 4. Basal leaf, x 1.

Ray flowers purple. Dry prairies. Western Minnesota, west of a line joining Jackson, Nicollet, Becker, and Clay counties.

COMPOSITAE. *Composite Family*

PHILADELPHIA FLEABANE (*Erigeron philadelphicus*).
Upper portion of stem, x 1.

Ray flowers in the head very numerous, 150 or more,
pale lavender, pink, or rarely white; stem leaves
clasping; perennial by basal offshoots. Moist, open
meadows, often in disturbed soil. Throughout
the state.

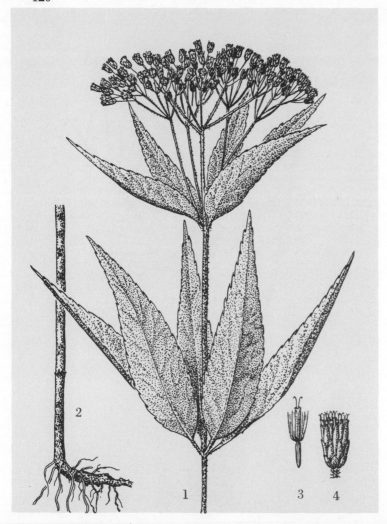

COMPOSITAE. Composite Family

JOE-PYE WEED (*Eupatorium maculatum*).

1. Upper section of stem, x ½. 2. Base of stem, x ½.
3. Disc flower, x 2. 4. Flowering head, x 2.

Flowers purple, about 12–20 per head; stems to 5 ft.
or more tall; plants perennial. Low, wet meadows
or open woods. Generally distributed throughout
the state. Four other kinds of *Eupatorium* occur in
Minnesota. One of them, also called Joe-Pye weed,
E. purpureum, is very similar to *E. maculatum* but
has only 3–8 flowers in each head. It is found in dryer
habitats in the eastern and north-central parts of
the state and is less common.

COMPOSITAE. *Composite Family*

WHITE SNAKEROOT (*Eupatorium rugosum*).

1. Upper part of stem, x 1. 2. Basal leaf, x 1.
3. Flowering head, x 2.

Flowers pure white, about 15–30 in each head; stems mostly 1.5–3.0 ft. tall; perennial from underground stems. Woods and thickets. In Minnesota, south and west of a line joining Chisago and Clay counties.

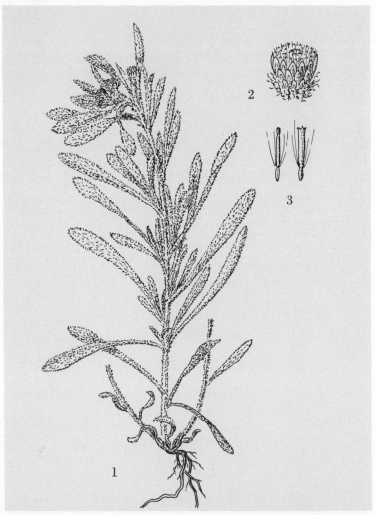

1

2

3

COMPOSITAE. *Composite Family*

LOW CUDWEED; EVERLASTING (*Gnaphalium uliginosum*).

1. Habit, x 1. 2. Flowering head, x 4. 3. Outer and inner flowers from the same head, x 4.

Clusters of flowering heads green or brownish. Low, damp, often disturbed areas; introduced from Europe and sometimes a weed here. Mostly in the central and northeastern parts of the state.

COMPOSITAE. Composite Family

GUMWEED; ROSINWEED (*Grindelia squarrosa*).

1. Upper half of the stem, x 1. 2. Middle section of stem, x 1.

Ray flowers yellow; stems mostly 1–2 ft. tall; bracts of flowering heads very sticky. Old fields, dry pastures, and prairies. Scattered records from all quarters of the state; probably present in most localities in the eastern half of the state by introduction.

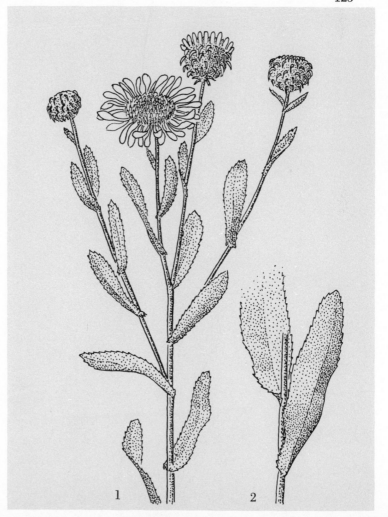

1   2

COMPOSITAE. Composite Family

SNEEZEWEED (*Helenium autumnale*).

1. Upper part of stem, x 1. 2. Middle section of stem with leaf base, x 1.

Ray flowers yellow; stems mostly 1.5–4.0 ft. tall, winged (flanged) from the bases of the leaves. Moist, low ground, meadows, and thickets. At scattered localities throughout the state, but rare in the northeastern quarter.

COMPOSITAE. *Composite Family*

COMMON SUNFLOWER (*Helianthus annuus*).

1. Upper part of stem, x 1. 2. Base of lower stem leaf, x 1. 3. Involucral bract, x 1.

Ray flowers yellow; surfaces of stems and leaves rough; plants annual, often weedy. Low, rich, often disturbed soil. Includes the cultivated sunflower which frequently escapes; these forms have larger and fewer heads. Generally distributed throughout the state but more frequent in the southern portions. We have 12 additional species of sunflowers native to the state; many of these are conspicuous components of the woods and prairie floras.

COMPOSITAE. Composite Family

OX-EYE (*Heliopsis helianthoides*).

Upper part of stem, x 1.

Ray flowers yellow; leaves paired along the stem, rough; stems mostly 1.5–4.0 ft. tall. Dry woods and prairies. Generally distributed throughout the state.

COMPOSITAE. *Composite Family*

BLUE LETTUCE; BLUE LACTUCA (*Lactuca pulchella*).
1. Upper part of plant, x 1. 2. Single flower from head, x 1. 3. Achene, x 1. 4. Middle and lower stem leaves, x 1.

Flowers blue or bluish-purple; stems mostly 1–2 ft. tall, arising from rootstocks; surfaces of stems and leaves bluish, usually completely smooth; juice milky. Moist, low places, prairies, and open woods. Generally distributed in the state, but rare in the northeastern quarter. Several other kinds of wild lettuce, some with yellow flowers, occur in Minnesota.

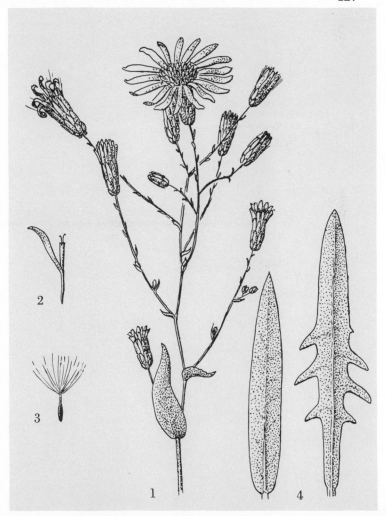

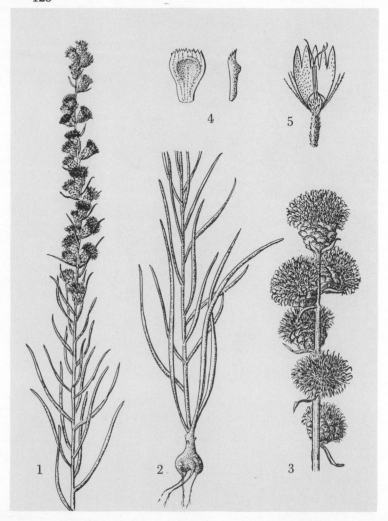

COMPOSITAE. *Composite Family*

BLAZING STAR (*Liatris aspera*).

1–2. Habit, x ¼. 3. Top of inflorescence, x 1. 4. Back and side view of involucral bract, x 2. 5. A single flower, the corolla opened to expose interior, x 2.

Flowers purple or sometimes white; stems stiffly erect, 1 or more together, usually 1–3 ft. tall. Dry, open places in woods or meadows, often in sandy soil. In Minnesota, south and west of a line joining Pine, Cass, and Kittson counties. We have 5 kinds of blazing stars in the state; some of the others are quite similar to this one.

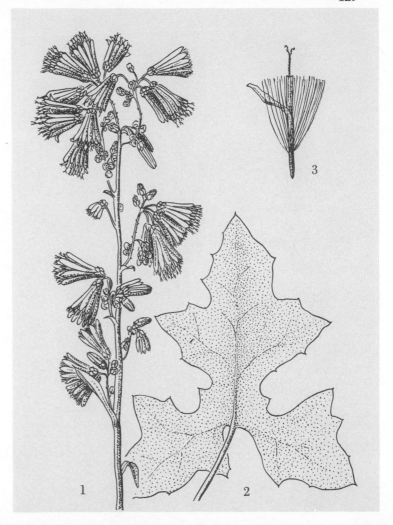

COMPOSITAE. *Composite Family*

RATTLESNAKE ROOT (*Prenanthes alba*).

1. Inflorescence, x 1. 2. Basal leaf, x 1. 3. A single flower from the head, x 2.

Flowers greenish or yellowish; stems mostly 1–3 ft. tall; both the stems and leaves bluish; juice milky; bristles of the achenes brown. Woods. Found generally around the state except in the southwestern corner.

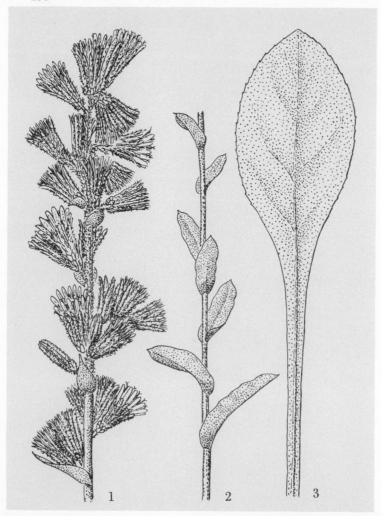

1. Top of inflorescence, x 1. 2. Middle section of stem, x ½. 3. Basal leaf, x ½.

COMPOSITAE. Composite Family

GLAUCOUS RATTLESNAKE ROOT (*Prenanthes racemosa*).

1. Top of inflorescence, x 1. 2. Middle section of stem, x ½. 3. Basal leaf, x ½.

Flowers of the heads pink or purplish; stems mostly 2–4 ft. tall, covered with hair near the top; stems and leaves bluish. Damp prairies. In Minnesota, south and west of a line joining Ramsey, Clay, and Roseau counties.

COMPOSITAE. *Composite Family*

PRAIRIE CONEFLOWER (*Ratibida columnifera*).

1. Flowering heads, x 1. 2. Base of plant, x 1. 3. Middle section of stem, x 1. 4. A single disc flower, x 4. 5. Bract attached at base of disc flower and clasping the achene, x 4.

Ray flowers yellow, less commonly partly yellow and purple or entirely purple; stems mostly 1–2 ft. tall. Dry prairies. Found at scattered localities in Minnesota south and west of a line joining Ramsey, Hubbard, and Kittson counties.

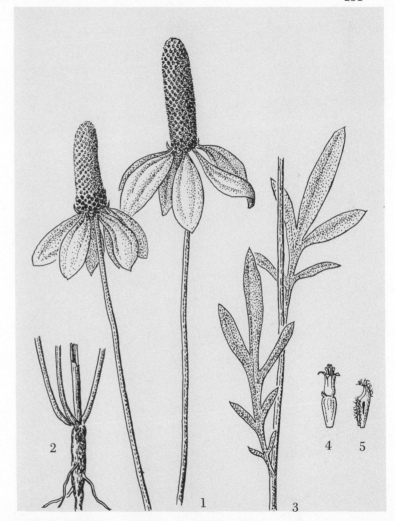

4   5

1   2   3

COMPOSITAE. *Composite Family*

CONEFLOWER (*Ratibida pinnata*).

1–2. Mature and immature flowering heads, x ¾.
3. Lower stem leaf, x ¾. 4. A single disc flower, x 4.
5. Bract attached at base of disc flower, x 4.

Ray flowers light yellow; stems mostly 1–3 ft. tall.
Prairies and dry woods. Southern and southeastern
Minnesota south of the Twin Cities.

COMPOSITAE. Composite Family

GOLDENGLOW (*Rudbeckia laciniata*).

1. Upper part of stem, x 1. 2–3. Upper and lower stem leaves, x ¼.

Ray flowers yellow; stems often to 6 ft. tall or more, smooth, bluish. Moist soil, low meadows, and borders; usually in full sun. At scattered localities over most of the state.

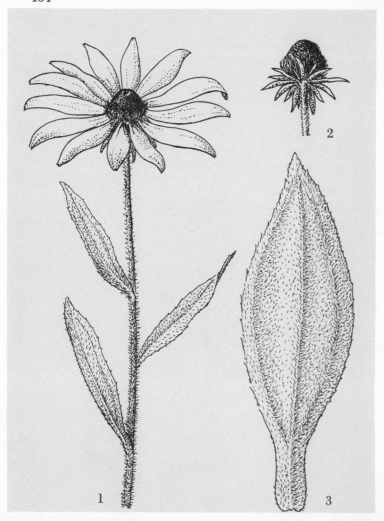

1

2

3

COMPOSITAE. Composite Family

BLACK-EYED SUSAN (*Rudbeckia serotina*).

1. Upper part of stem, x ¾. 2. Immature flowering head, x ¾. 3. Middle stem leaf, x ¾.

Ray flowers orange-yellow in ours; stems mostly 1–2 ft. tall; stems and leaves covered with stiff hairs. Dry, sunny meadows, prairies, and margins of woods, often in disturbed soil. Throughout the state.

COMPOSITAE. Composite Family

GOLDEN RAGWORT; SWAMP SQUAW-WEED (*Senecio aureus*).

1. Upper part of stem, x 1. 2. Middle stem leaf, x 1. 3. Basal leaf, x 1.

Ray flowers golden-yellow; stems mostly 1–2 ft. tall; spreading by rootstocks. Wet, swampy woods and meadows. Found in most parts of the state. Six or 7 kinds of ragwort are native to Minnesota.

136

COMPOSITAE. *Composite Family*

PRAIRIE RAGWORT (*Senecio plattensis*).

1. Upper part of stem, x 1. 2. Middle or lower stem leaf, x 1. 3. Basal leaf, x 1.

Ray flowers yellow; stems mostly 1–2 ft. tall, thick wool at the base even when old. Mostly in dry, open prairies. Found over most of the state, but commonest in the west. A very similar ragwort, *S. pauperculus*, is encountered more frequently in eastern Minnesota. It differs chiefly in being less woolly at the base of the stem and even this is usually lost as the stems grow older.

COMPOSITAE. *Composite Family*

COMPASS-PLANT; ROSINWEED (*Silphium laciniatum*).

1. Inflorescence, x ⅓. 2. Basal or lower stem leaf, x ⅓.

Ray flowers yellow; stems mostly 2–8 ft. tall, the surfaces of the stems and leaves covered with rough hair; lower leaves tending to be upright or vertical with the edges aligned in a north and south direction. Rich prairies. In southeastern Minnesota from a line connecting Ramsey and Blue Earth counties; also reported from Lincoln County.

138

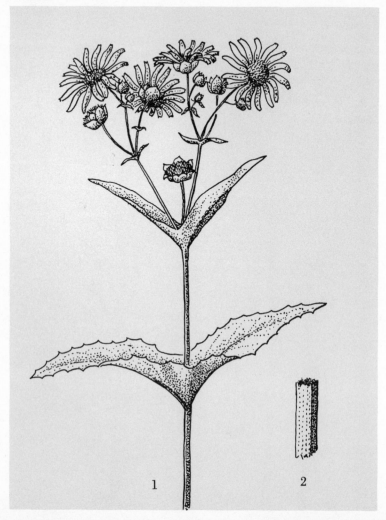

1. 2.

COMPOSITAE. *Composite Family*

CUP-PLANT (*Silphium perfoliatum*).

1. Upper part of stem, x ⅓. 2. Short section of stem, x 1.

Ray flowers yellow; stems mostly 2–6 ft. tall, square, nearly smooth, the stem leaves paired and joined together (as shown). Rich woods and prairies. In Minnesota south of a line joining Ramsey, Hennepin, Nicollet, and Lincoln counties.

COMPOSITAE. Composite Family

TALL GOLDENROD (*Solidago altissima*).

1. Upper half of stem, x ¼. 2. Stem leaf, x 1.
3. Flowering head, x 2.

Flowers yellow; stems often 3–5 ft. tall, usually quite
hairy. Low places, meadows, and thickets. Found
throughout the state and difficult to distinguish from
several similar species except by technical differences.

GRAY GOLDENROD (*Solidago nemoralis*).

4. Habit, x ¼. 5. Upper and lower stem leaves,
x 1. 6. Flowering head, x 2.

Flowers yellow; stems usually 1–2 ft. tall, both the
stems and leaves densely covered with grayish hairs.
Dry soil, open woods, hillsides, and pastures.
Throughout the state. There are about 20 species
of goldenrods in Minnesota.

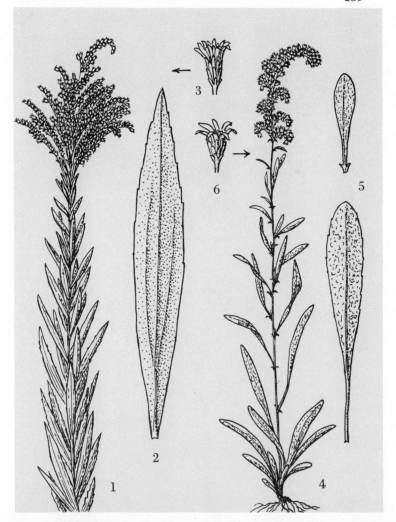

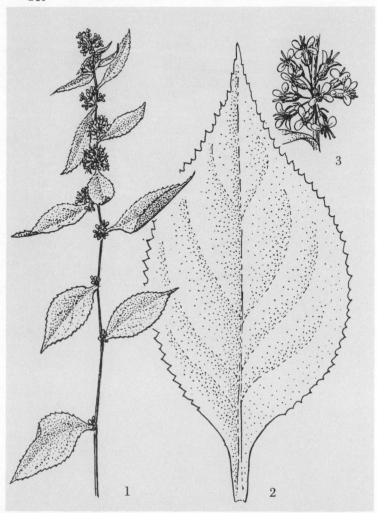

COMPOSITAE. *Composite Family*

ZIG-ZAG GOLDENROD (*Solidago flexicaulis*).

1. Upper part of stem, x ¼. 2. Lower stem leaf, x 1. 3. Part of inflorescence, x 1.

Flowers yellow; stems usually 1.0–2.5 ft. tall, zig-zag, smooth or nearly so. Woods and thickets. Widely distributed in the state but apparently absent in the northern fifth and rare or absent in the southwestern corner.

COMPOSITAE. Composite Family

GRASS-LEAVED GOLDENROD (*Solidago graminifolia*).

1. Uppermost part of stem, x 1. 2. Upper half of stem, x ¼.

Flowers yellow; plants reproducing vigorously by underground stems; flowering stems mostly 2–4 ft. tall. Margins of woods or open ground. Generally distributed throughout the state.

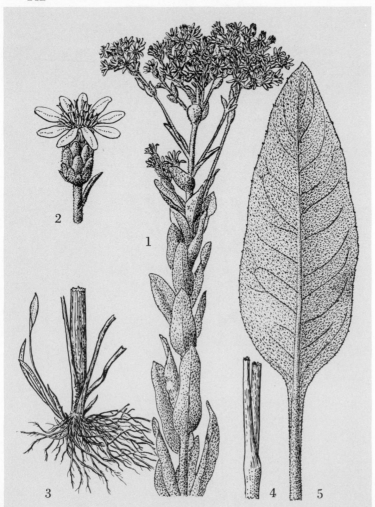

COMPOSITAE. *Composite Family*

STIFF GOLDENROD (*Solidago rigida*).

1. Upper half of stem, x ½. 2. A single flowering
head, x 2. 3. Base of plant, x ¼. 4–5. Lower
stem leaf, x ½.

Flowers yellow; stems usually 1.5–4.0 ft. tall, both
the stem and leaves covered with short hair; flowering heads close together, forming a dense, flat-topped
cluster at the top of the stem. Dry prairies and edges
of thickets. Throughout the state.

COMPOSITAE. *Composite Family*

GOAT'S-BEARD (*Tragopogon dubius*).

1. Flowering head, x ½. 2. Base of plant and root, x ½. 3. Ripened head, x ½. 4. Achene, x 1.

Flowers greenish-yellow; peduncle much enlarged just below the flowering head; juice milky; biennial. Open, moist to dry sites. Introduced from Europe and now fully established throughout the state. Another goat's-beard, *T. pratensis*, also introduced from Europe, is found in Minnesota but is not so frequent. It differs chiefly in having a more slender peduncle and shorter involucral bracts.

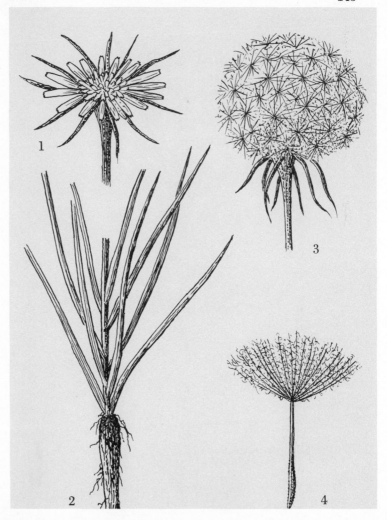

COMPOSITAE. Composite Family

WESTERN IRONWEED (*Vernonia fasciculata*).
1. Upper part of stem, x ½. 2. Stem leaf, x ½.
3. Flowering head, x 2.

Flowers in the head all alike and tubular, purple; plants mostly 2–4 ft. tall, smooth, the stems often red or purplish. Wet prairies. Common in the southern third of the state; in the west seen as far north as Kittson County and in the east to St. Louis County.

CONVOLVULACEAE. Morning-glory Family

FIELD BINDWEED (*Convolvulus arvensis*).

1. Part of stem, x 1. 2. Capsule enclosed in calyx, x 2.

Corolla white to pink; stems trailing or climbing, up to 3 or 4 ft. long. Common weed in old fields, road margins, and waste places; introduced from Europe. Met with in the southern and western two-fifths of the state, south of a line joining Hennepin, Grant, and Clay counties.

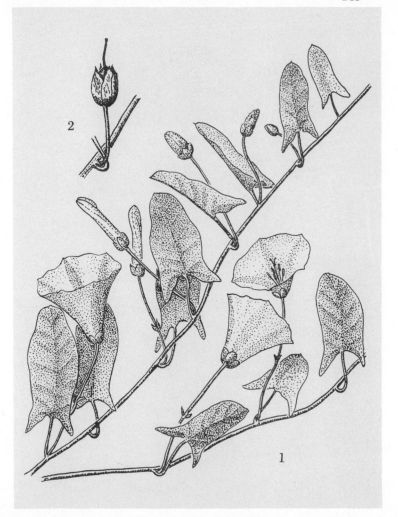

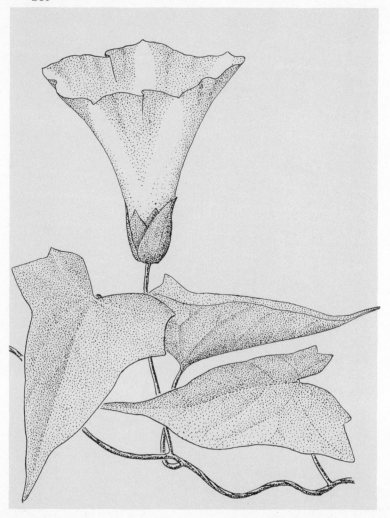

CONVOLVULACEAE. Morning-glory Family

HEDGE BINDWEED; WILD MORNING-GLORY
(*Convolvulus sepium*).

Short section of stem with typical leaves
and flower, x 1.

Corolla white or pink; stems twining or trailing,
up to 10 ft. long. Thickets, shorelines, roadsides,
and waste places; both native and introduced from
Europe. Found throughout the state.

CONVOLVULACEAE. *Morning-glory Family*

UPRIGHT BINDWEED (*Convolvulus spithamaeus*).

Upper part of stem, x 1.

Corolla white or pink; stems simple or a little branched, erect to the flowers, the tip sometimes drooping but not truly twining, rarely to 1.5 ft. tall. Dry, often sandy soil, fields, or open woods. In Minnesota, northeast of a line joining Houston, Hennepin, Cass, Clearwater, and Roseau counties.

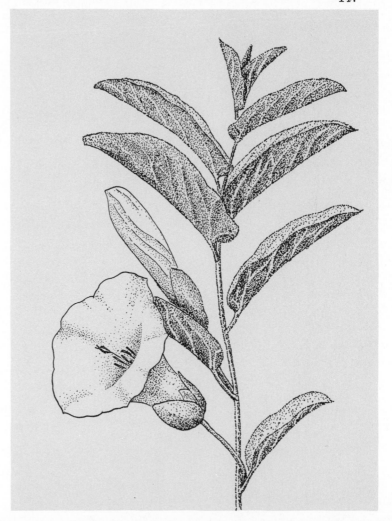

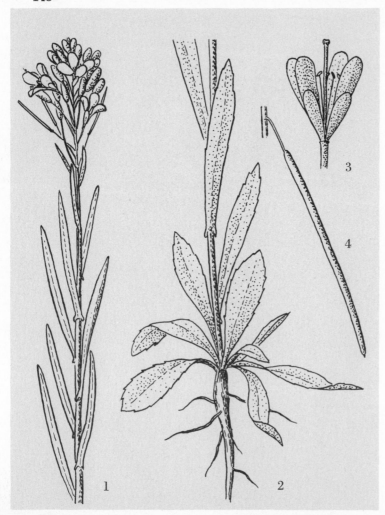

1

2

3

4

CRUCIFERAE. Mustard Family

PINK ROCK CRESS (*Arabis divaricarpa*).

1–2. Habit, x 1. 3. Flower, x 2. 4. Seed pod, x 1.

Petals white or more commonly pink or purplish; stems mostly 1.0–2.5 ft. tall; seed pods, when mature, widely spreading; biennial. Sandy soil, in full sun. Throughout the state.

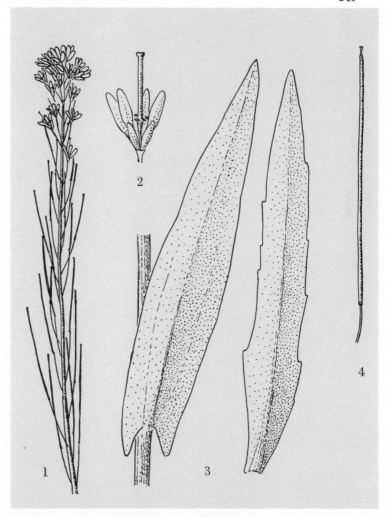

CRUCIFERAE. Mustard Family

TOWER MUSTARD (*Arabis glabra*).

1. Inflorescence, x 1. 2. Flower, x 2. 3. Middle and lowermost stem leaves, x 1. 4. Seed pod, x 1.

Petals creamy or yellowish; stems mostly 1.5–3.5 ft. tall, slightly hairy near the bottom, smooth in the middle and upper parts, the stem and leaves bluish; seed pods, when mature, erect or nearly so; biennial. Dry, often sandy areas, pastures and edges of woods, sometimes a weed. North-central, northeastern, and eastern Minnesota; also in Kittson County.

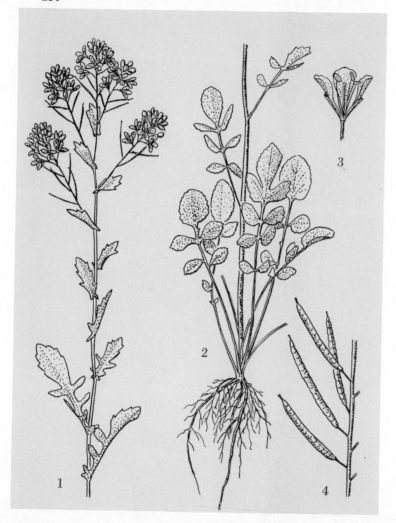

1

2

3

4

CRUCIFERAE. *Mustard Family*

COMMON WINTER CRESS; YELLOW ROCKET (*Barbarea vulgaris*).

1–2. Habit, x ½. 3. Flower, x 2. 4. Mature seed pods, x 1.

Petals bright yellow; stems smooth. Weed in meadows, fields, and roadsides; introduced from Europe. Seen mostly in the eastern half of the state.

CRUCIFERAE. *Mustard Family*

HOARY ALYSSUM (*Berteroa incana*).

1–2. Habit, x ½. 3. Flower, x 2. 4. Seed pod, x 2.

Petals white; stems and leaves ashy-gray as a result of the dense cover of fine, branched hairs; annual. Fields, roadsides, and waste places; weedy; introduced from Europe. Widely distributed in the state except in the southwestern counties and in the middle counties along the Canadian border.

152

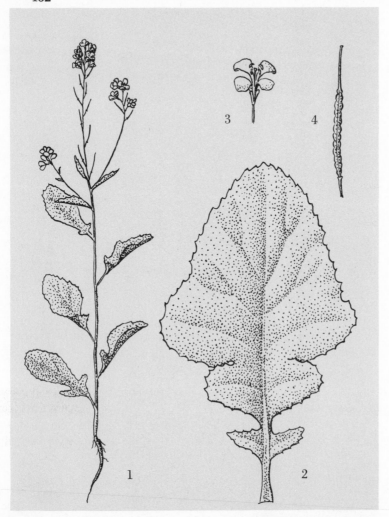

CRUCIFERAE. *Mustard Family*

CHARLOCK; MUSTARD (*Brassica kaber*).

1. Habit, x ¼. 2. Lower stem leaf, x 1. 3. Flower, x 1. 4. Seed pod, x 1.

Petals yellow; stems and leaves usually covered with rough hair; annual. Disturbed ground, roadsides, and cultivated or uncultivated fields; weedy; introduced from Europe. Throughout the state.

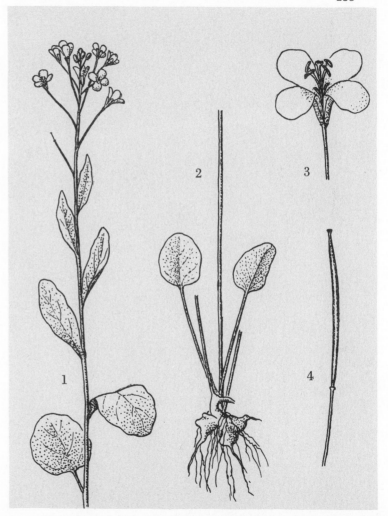

CRUCIFERAE. Mustard Family

SPRING CRESS (*Cardamine bulbosa*).

1–2. Habit, x ½. 3. Flower, x 2. 4. Seed pod, x 2.

Petals white; stems and leaves smooth. Around springs and in wet meadows and woods. In southern and western Minnesota, south and west of a line joining southern Pine, southern Beltrami, and Kittson counties. Three other kinds of *Cardamine*, all known as bitter cress, occur in the state.

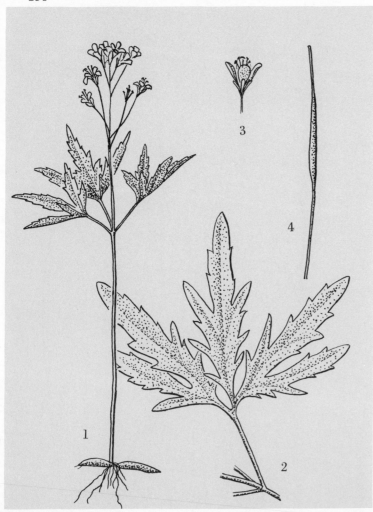

CRUCIFERAE. *Mustard Family*

TOOTHWORT (*Dentaria laciniata*).

1. Habit, x ½. 2. Division of the leaf, x 1.
3. Flower, x 1. 4. Seed pod, x 1.

Petals white or purplish. Moist, rich woods. In the state, present to the south and east of a line joining southern St. Louis, Morrison, and Blue Earth counties; also in Murray County.

CRUCIFERAE. *Mustard Family*

DRABA (*Draba reptans*).

1. Habit, x 1. 2. Flower, x 2. 3. Leaf, x 2.

Petals white; diminutive annual. Dry, often sandy, disturbed soil of pastures and rocky outcrops. In southern Minnesota south of Hennepin County, and in the border counties along the western edge of the state.

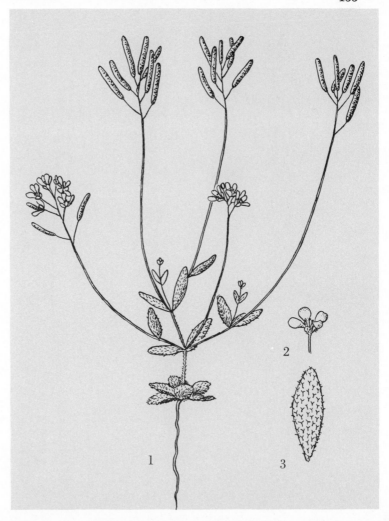

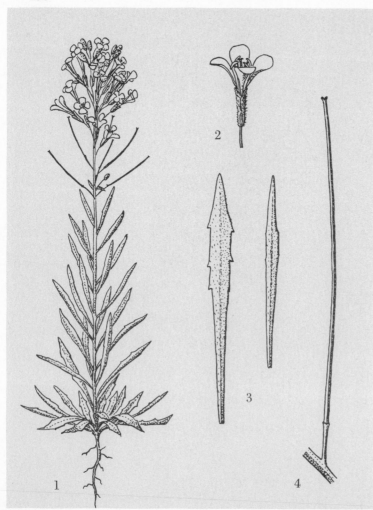

CRUCIFERAE. *Mustard Family*

WESTERN WALLFLOWER (*Erysimum asperum*).

1. Habit, x ⅓. 2. Flower, x 1. 3. Lower and middle stem leaves, x 1. 4. Seed pod, x 1.

Petals yellow to orange-yellow; leaves and stems grayish because of the closely spaced, branched surface hairs. Dry prairies and eroded areas. Found along a diagonal band joining Ramsey and Clay counties; also in southern Lake County. Present in some of the reported localities by introduction from farther west. Two other kinds of *Erysimum*, both less attractive but more widely distributed, occur in the state.

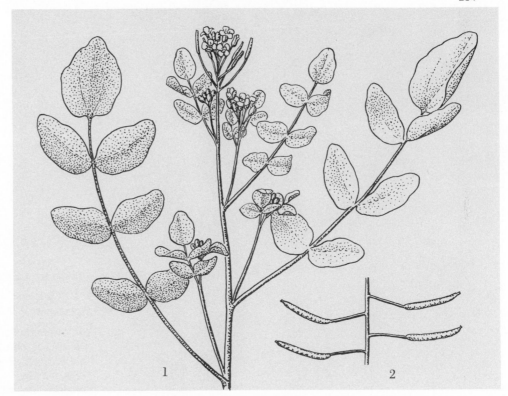

1

2

*CRUCIFERAE. Mustard
Family*

WATER CRESS (*Nasturtium
officinale*).

1. Upper part of stem, x 1. 2. Seed
pods, x 1.

Petals white; stems submerged or
partly floating, producing roots at
the nodes, the stems and leaves smooth. Clear springs and streams; introduced from
Europe, but now appearing naturalized in many places. In southeastern Minnesota
east of a line joining Carver, Rice, and Fillmore counties; also in Hubbard County.

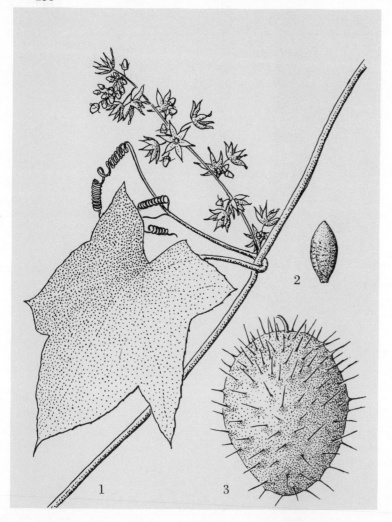

CUCURBITACEAE. Gourd Family

WILD CUCUMBER (*Echinocystis lobata*).

1. Joint of stem with leaf, tendril, and male inflorescence, x 1. 2. Seed, x 1. 3. Ripe seed pod, x 1.

Flowers greenish-white, unisexual, the male in large, branched clusters, the female inconspicuous and only 1, at a given joint of the stem; annual, the stems often many feet long, climbing by tendrils; fruits bladderlike. Clambering over low shrubbery at edges of woods, along fence rows, etc., in rich, moist soil. Found throughout the state.

CUCURBITACEAE. *Gourd Family*

BUR CUCUMBER (*Sicyos angulatus*).

1. Joint of stem with leaf, tendril, and a cluster each of female and male flowers, x 1. 2. Cluster of ripe seed pods, x 1.

Flowers greenish or white, unisexual, the male in a loose, elongate cluster, the female in a stalked spherical cluster; seeds 1 in each pod; stems often many feet long, climbing by tendrils; annual, from seed each year. Forest borders, stream banks, etc., moist, rich soil. Occurring sporadically in Minnesota south of a line joining Hennepin and Big Stone counties; also near Ponemah in Beltrami County.

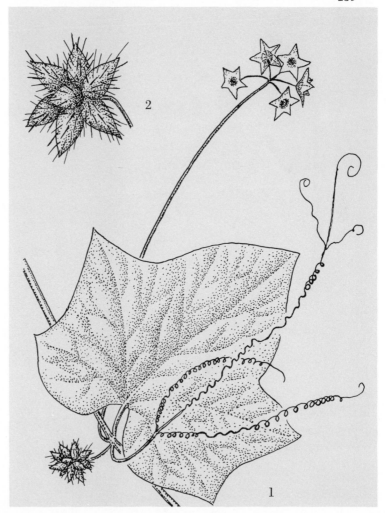

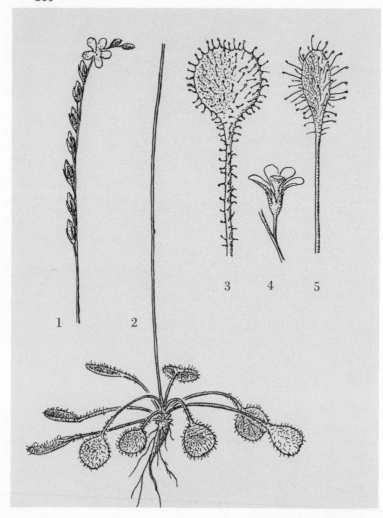

1   2

3   4   5

DROSERACEAE. *Sundew Family*

ROUND-LEAVED SUNDEW (*Drosera rotundifolia*).

1–2. Habit, x 1. 3. Leaf, x 2. 4. Flower, x 2.

Petals white to pink. Hummocks in sphagnum bogs or, especially, on moss-covered, partially sunken logs in small ponds. Central and northeastern Minnesota, north and east of a line connecting Blue Earth, Pope, southeastern Clearwater, and Lake of the Woods counties; commonest in the coniferous zone.

OBLONG-LEAVED SUNDEW (*Drosera intermedia*).

5. Leaf, x 2.

Wet meadows, bogs, or shallow water. Principally in the northeastern quarter of the state.

EUPHORBIACEAE. *Spurge Family*

FLOWERING SPURGE (*Euphorbia corollata*).

1. Upper half of the stem, x ¼. 2. Branch, x 1.
3. Fruit, x 1.

Flower clusters white; stems to 3 ft. tall, 1 or more from the crown of a thick, deep, perennial root; juice milky. Open woods and old fields. Southeastern Minnesota, east of a line joining Pine, Carver, Rice, and Fillmore counties; also in Renville County.

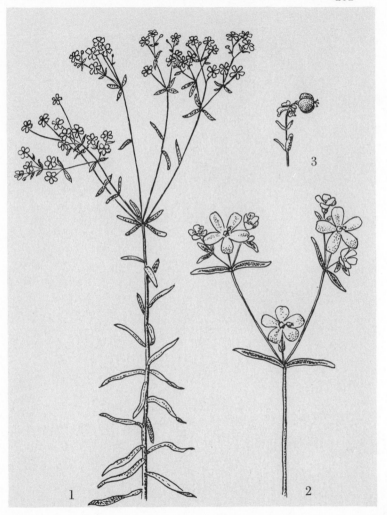

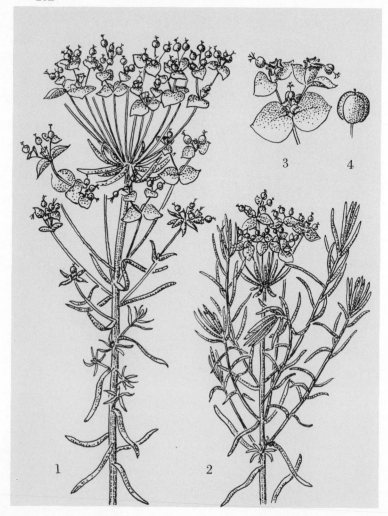

3   4

EUPHORBIACEAE. *Spurge Family*

CYPRESS SPURGE (*Euphorbia cyparissias*).

1–2. Top part of plant; 2 stages, x 1. 3. Ultimate branch, x 2. 4. Fruit, x 2.

Floral leaves and bracts yellowish when young; stems tufted, mostly 1.0–1.5 ft. tall; spreading by means of a deep, perennial underground rootstock; juice milky. Introduced into cemeteries and gardens and spreading into roadsides, old fields, and meadows; from Europe. Common in southeastern Minnesota and occasionally seen northward in the state.

EUPHORBIACEAE. *Spurge Family*

LEAFY SPURGE (*Euphorbia esula*).

1. Upper part of plant, x ¾. 2. Stem bases and root-stock, x ⅔. 3. Leaf, x 1. 4. Inflorescence in flower, x 3. 5. Fruit, x 3.

Floral leaves and bracts yellowish-green; stem 1 or a few together, mostly 1.5–2.5 ft. tall; arising from a deep, extensively spreading, underground root-stock; juice milky. Sandy, dry fields and hillsides; introduced from Europe but fully naturalized. Generally distributed in the state, especially in the south and west; occasionally occurs northeastward.

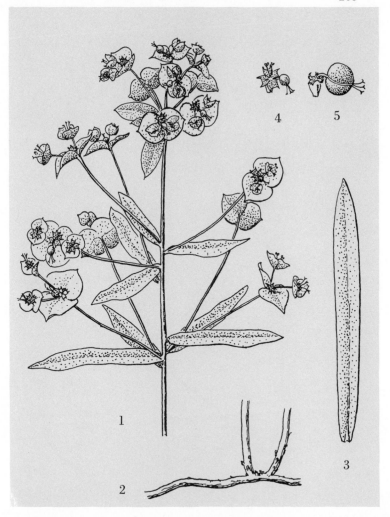

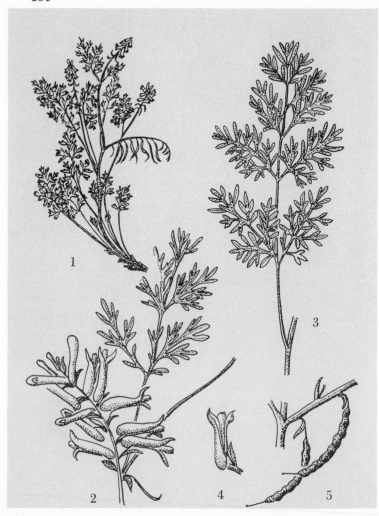

FUMARIACEAE. Fumitory Family

GOLDEN CORYDALIS (*Corydalis aurea*).

1. One branch from the crown, x ¼. 2. Inflorescence, x 1. 3. Stem leaf, x 1. 4. Flower, x 1. 5. Fruits, x 1.

Corolla bright yellow; stems 0.5–1.5 ft. long, reclining at the base, 1 to many from the crown, smooth, both the stems and leaves bluish; annual or biennial. Disturbed, moist soil, old fields, banks, forest openings, etc. Throughout the state, but rare in the prairie areas.

FUMARIACEAE. Fumitory Family

PALE CORYDALIS (*Corydalis sempervirens*).

1. Habit, x ¼. 2. Inflorescence, x 1. 3. Fruits, x 1.
4. Stem leaf, x 1.

Corolla pink or purplish with a yellow tip; stems
mostly 1.0–2.5 ft. tall, the stems and leaves smooth,
very blue; annual or biennial. Rocky outcrops,
shorelines, disturbed soil, forest openings, etc.
Northern and eastern Minnesota, northeast of a line
joining Chisago, Mille Lacs, Clearwater, and Lake
of the Woods counties.

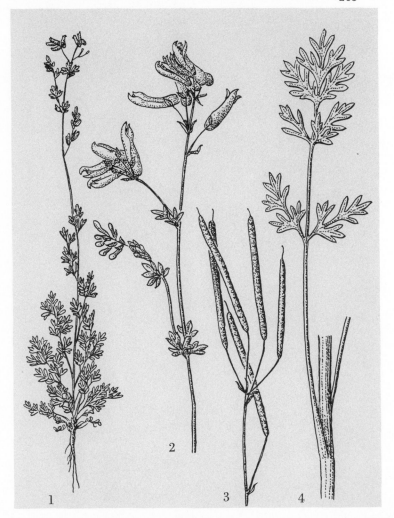

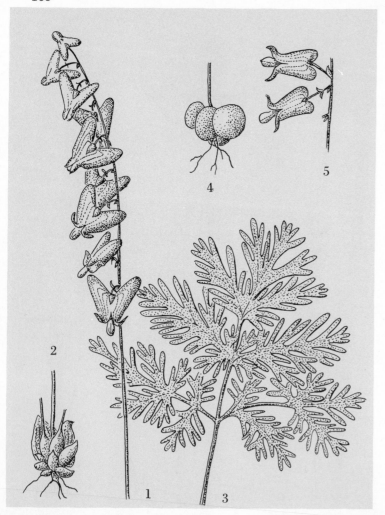

4

5

2

1

3

FUMARIACEAE. *Fumitory Family*

DUTCHMAN'S BREECHES (*Dicentra cucullaria*).

1. Inflorescence, x 1. 2. Bulblets, x 1. 3. Leaf, x 1.

Corolla white or pinkish, tipped with cream, both the flowers and leaves ephemeral; stems smooth, arising from a cluster of white or pinkish, shallowly buried bulblets. In deep, organic soil and rich woods. Over the entire state except in the northwestern and Canadian border areas.

SQUIRREL CORN (*Dicentra canadensis*).

4. Bulblets, x 1. 5. Flowers, x 1.

Similar, but with the petal spurs very short and the bulblets spherical and yellow. In Minnesota, known only from Winona County.

GENTIANACEAE. Gentian Family

CLOSED GENTIAN; BOTTLE GENTIAN (*Gentiana andrewsii*).

1. Upper part of plant, x ½. 2. Flower, the corolla opened to expose stamens and pistil, x 1. 3. Capsule, x 1.

Flowers bluish-white to bluish-purple; stems 1–2 ft. tall. Wet meadows, woods, prairies, and shores. Generally distributed throughout Minnesota. Ten additional species of wild gentians have been reported in Minnesota. Some of them are similar to this one.

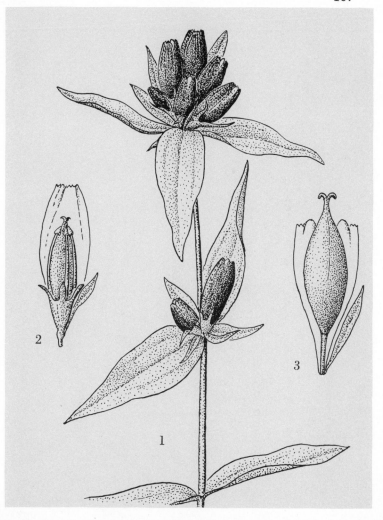

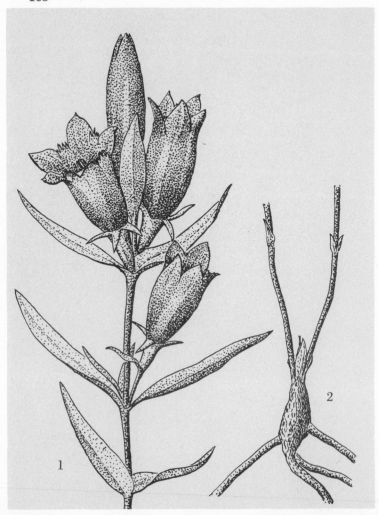

1

2

GENTIANACEAE. *Gentian Family*

PRAIRIE GENTIAN (*Gentiana puberula*).

1. Upper part of plant, x 1. 2. Base of plant, x 1.

Flowers blue or bluish-purple. Stems 0.5–1.5 ft. tall. Dry upland woods and prairies. Generally distributed south and west of a line joining Washington, northern Mille Lacs, and Kittson counties.

GENTIANACEAE. *Gentian Family*

SPURRED GENTIAN (*Halenia deflexa*).

1–2. Habit, x 1. 3. Capsule, x 1.

Flowers purplish or green; annual. The spur is the pocket formed by the base of each of the 4 petals. In wet woods and along shores, in partial sun. In northeastern Minnesota, north and east of a line connecting Carlton, southeastern Clearwater, and Kittson counties; commonest in the coniferous zone.

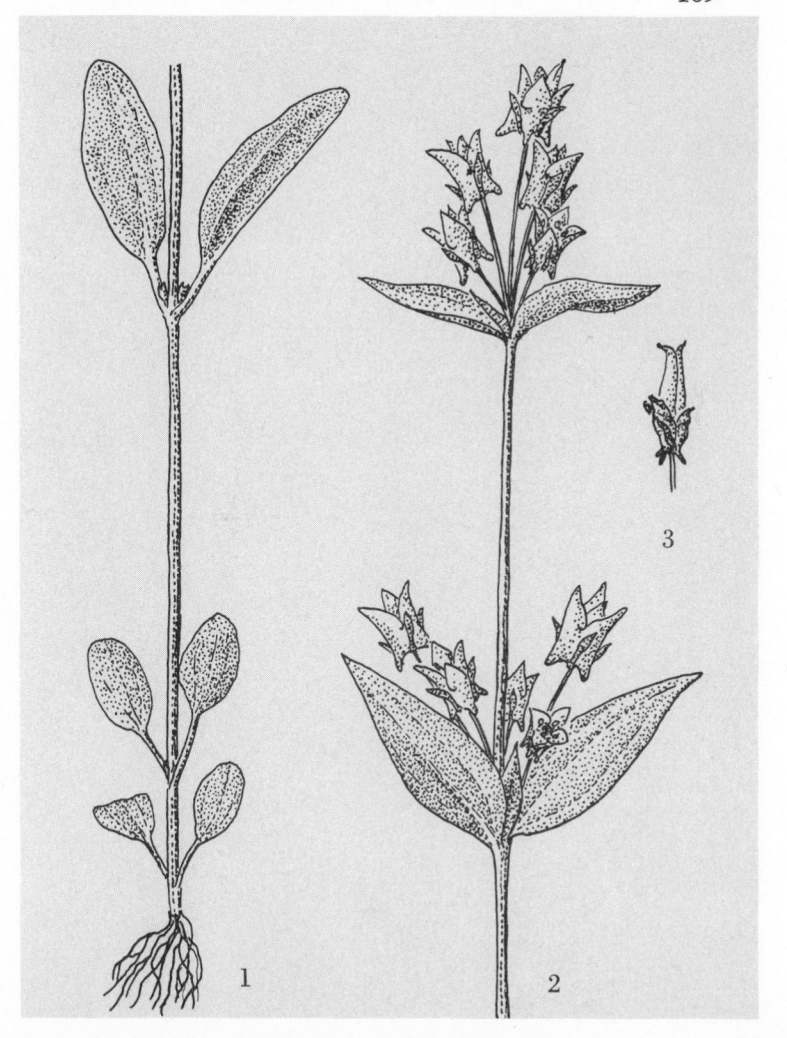

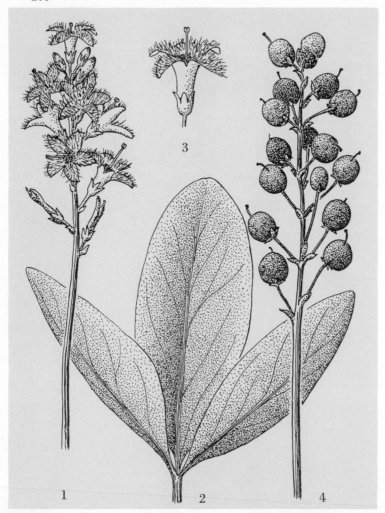

1

3

2

4

GENTIANACEAE. *Gentian Family*

BUCKBEAN; BOGBEAN (*Menyanthes trifoliata*).

1. Inflorescence, x 1. 2. Leaf blade, x 1. 3. Flower, x 1½. 4. Inflorescence, in fruit, x 1.

Petals white or pinkish; leaves crowded at the base of the flowering stem; flowering stems usually less than 1 ft. high; perennial from a thick, creeping rootstock. Sphagnum bogs, sedge mats, and lake margins. Goodhue, Waseca, and Blue Earth counties north to the Canadian border; westward in Minnesota to a line joining McLeod, Otter Tail, Clearwater, and Lake of the Woods counties.

GERANIACEAE. *Geranium Family*

BICKNELL'S GERANIUM (*Geranium bicknellii*).

1. Upper part of plant, x 1. 2. Capsule after seed dispersal, x 1.

Flowers pinkish-purple; stems mostly 1.0–1.5 ft. tall, covered with spreading hairs; annual or biennial. Disturbed soil in open woods and fields. Found over the entire state except for the southern and south-western two-fifths; rare in the west and northwest.

1

2

GERANIACEAE. Geranium Family

WILD GERANIUM; SPOTTED CRANESBILL (*Geranium maculatum*).

1. Upper part of plant, x ½. 2. Capsule after seed dispersal, x 1.

Flowers rose-purple or occasionally white; stems 1–2 ft. tall, from a thickened, perennial underground rhizome; basal leaves with long stalks, deeply cut. Woods, thickets, and adjacent meadows. Found throughout southeastern and central Minnesota and to Lake, Beltrami, and Clay counties in the north and west.

HYDROPHYLLACEAE. *Waterleaf Family*

VIRGINIA WATERLEAF (*Hydrophyllum virginianum*).
Upper part of stem, x 1.

Corolla lavender to white; stems 1–2 ft. tall. Rich,
damp woods. Found throughout southern and central Minnesota north to southern St. Louis County,
Lower Red Lake in Clearwater County, and western
Polk County. Another species, the appendaged
waterleaf, *H. appendiculatum*, is also found in southeastern Minnesota, from Goodhue County southward
and from Blue Earth County eastward. It has palmately lobed stem leaves and, also, the floral calyx
has an extra reflexed lobe between each of the
main lobes.

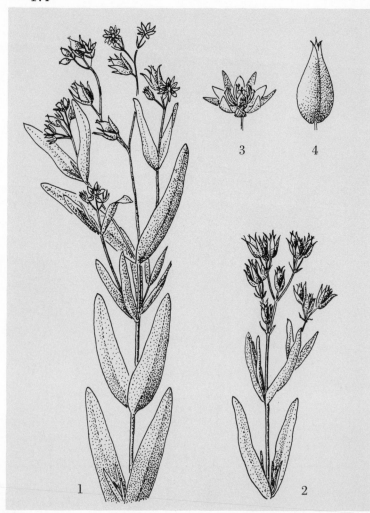

3

4

1

2

HYPERICACEAE. *St. John's-wort Family*

ST. JOHN'S-WORT (*Hypericum majus*).

1. Upper part of stem, x 1. 2. Branch bearing mature capsules, x 1. 3. Flower, x 3. 4. Capsule, x 3.

Petals yellow; stems 0.5–1.5 ft. tall. Wet meadows and shores. Most common in the northeastern two-fifths of the state from the Twin Cities northward; rare in the southeast and northwest; not recorded in the southwestern corner of the state. The common name is equally suitable for the other half-dozen species of *Hypericum* found in the state.

HYPERICACEAE. St. John's-wort Family

COMMON ST. JOHN'S-WORT (*Hypericum perforatum*).

1. Upper part of plant, x 1. 2. Branch with mature capsules, x 1.

Petals bright yellow; stems 1.0–2.5 ft. tall, 1 or more from the perennial crown. Old fields and pastures; a very attractive flower, introduced from Europe, now becoming a noxious weed. Common in the eastern third of the state, from Houston and Freeborn counties to Lake County; spreading rapidly and can be expected elsewhere.

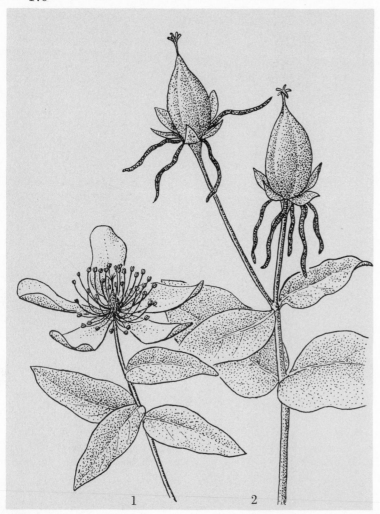

1   2

HYPERICACEAE. St. John's-wort Family

GREAT ST. JOHN'S-WORT (*Hypericum pyramidatum*).
1. Flowering branch, x 1. 2. Mature capsules, x 1.

Petals yellow; stems 1.5–5.0 ft. tall, succulent. Rich, moist soil, thickets, and meadows. Distributed in the eastern half of the state east of a line joining Brown, Morrison, and St. Louis counties. Quite the finest of our native St. John's-worts.

LABIATAE. Mint Family

FRAGRANT GIANT HYSSOP (*Agastache foeniculum*).

1. Top of stem with inflorescence, x 1. 2. Middle section of stem, x 1.

Flowers blue or purplish; stems 2–3 ft. tall; leaves bluish or whitish underneath; herbage with the odor of licorice when lightly crushed. Open, upland woods and prairies. Found throughout the state.

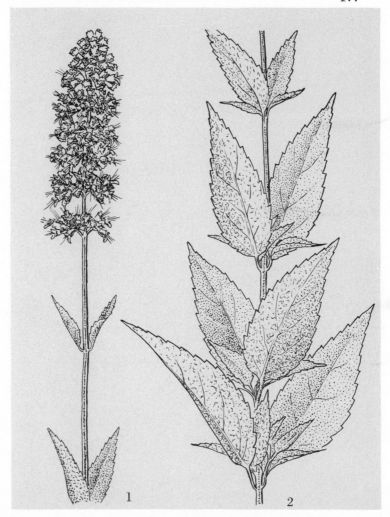

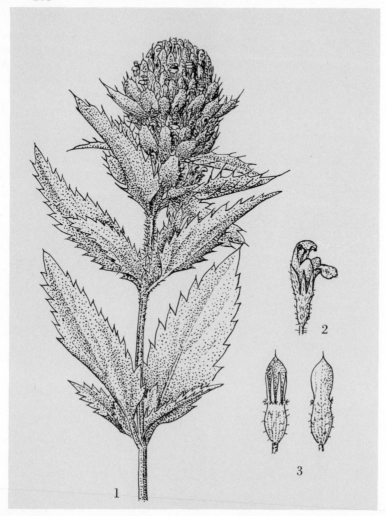

1

2

3

LABIATAE. Mint Family

DRAGONHEAD (*Dracocephalum parviflorum*).

1. Upper part of stem, x 1. 2. Flower, x 2. 3. Calyx viewed from front and back, x 2.

Flowers light blue to purple; stems 0.5–2.5 ft. tall; annual or biennial. In dry soil, often in old fields or clearings. Occasionally seen in all major areas of the state.

LABIATAE. Mint Family

GROUND IVY; GILL-OVER-THE-GROUND (*Glechoma hederacea*).

Outer part of stem, x 1.

Flowers purplish or bluish; stems trailing over the ground and rooting at the nodes; leaves green or often purplish, especially beneath. Damp, shaded places, yards, wood lots, and flood plains; naturalized from Europe. Of irregular occurrence in the state and still unrecorded from large areas in the northeast and southwest; often common elsewhere.

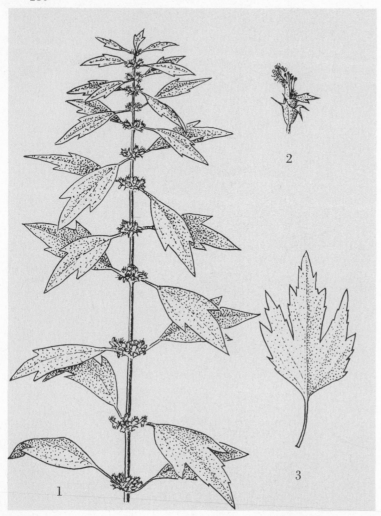

LABIATAE. *Mint Family*

MOTHERWORT (*Leonurus cardiaca*).

1. Upper part of stem, x ½. 2. Flower, x 2.
3. Lower stem leaf, x ½.

Flowers pale purple; stems 1.5–5.0 ft. tall; perennial with 1 to several annual stems from the crown. Occasional weed in rich, organic soil; introduced from Eurasia. Recorded from the southern half of the state from Morrison County southward; also in Wilkin, Clay, and Kittson counties and to be expected elsewhere.

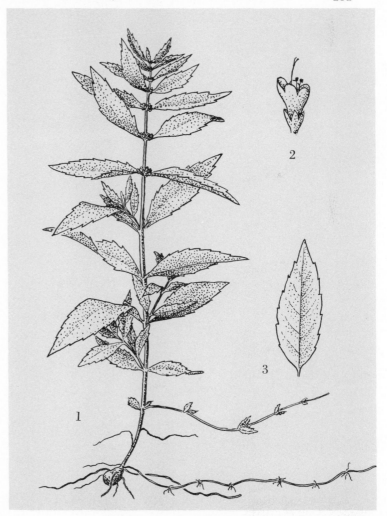

LABIATAE. Mint Family

NORTHERN BUGLEWEED (*Lycopus uniflorus*).

1. Habit, x ½. 2. Flower, x 4. 3. Leaf, x ½.

Flowers white. Spreading by runners; herbage not fragrant. Low, wet ground, streamsides and meadows. Found over most of the state, but commonest in the east-central and northeastern counties.

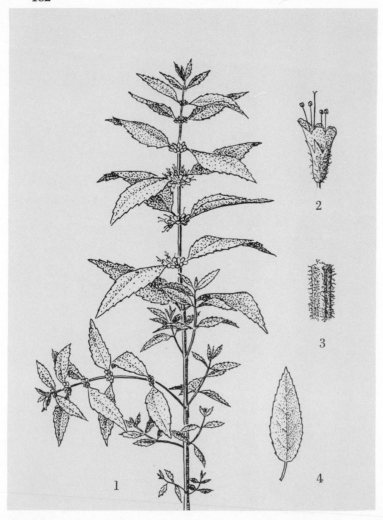

1

2

3

4

LABIATAE. Mint Family

FIELD MINT (*Mentha arvensis*).

1. Upper part of stem, x ½. 2. Flower, x 4.
3. Section of stem, x 2. 4. Leaf, x ½.

Flowers white, light pink, or purplish; stems 0.5–2.0 ft. tall, angled; spreading by runners; herbage very fragrant. Moist or wet places, especially along streams and lakeshores. Common throughout the state. This is our only native *Mentha*; others, all of European origin, are grown in gardens and sometimes persist without cultivation.

LABIATAE. Mint Family

WILD BERGAMOT; HORSEMINT (*Monarda fistulosa*).

1. Upper half of stem, x ½. 2. Lower stem leaf, x 1. 3. Flower, x 2. 4. Interior of calyx and young ovary, x 2.

Flowers pale lavender, pink, or rarely white; stems mostly 1.5–3.5 ft. tall, few to many from the same crown, the stems and leaves covered with gray hair to a greater or lesser extent; herbage exuding a strong, characteristic odor. In upland woods, meadows, and prairies. Found in southern and western Minnesota, south and west of a line joining Pine, Douglas, and Mahnomen counties.

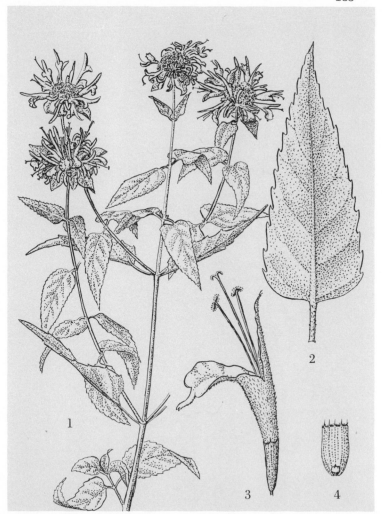

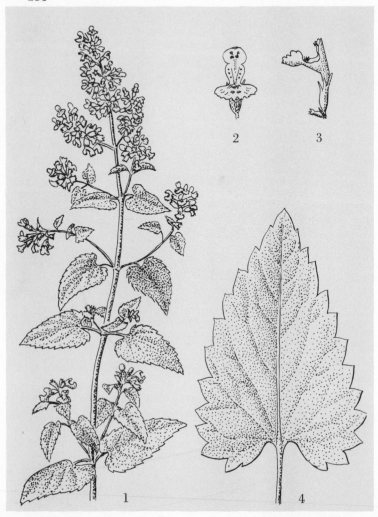

2

3

1

4

LABIATAE. Mint Family

CATNIP (*Nepeta cataria*).

1. Upper half of stem, x ½. 2. Face view of flower, x 2. 3. Side view of flower, x 2. 4. Lower stem leaf, x 1.

Flowers dull white, the lower lobe on the corolla dotted with purple; stems mostly 1.0–2.5 ft. tall, angled; herbage strongly and pleasantly fragrant; short-lived perennial. In waste areas, disturbed soil around dwellings, farmsteads, and fields; introduced from Europe. Generally distributed in the state south and west of a line joining southern St. Louis, Benton, Clay and Kittson counties.

LABIATAE. Mint Family

FALSE DRAGONHEAD (*Physostegia virginiana*).

1. Upper part of stem, x ½. 2. Face view of flower, x 1. 3. Side view of flower, x 1. 4. Lower stem leaf, x 1.

Flowers purple or lavender, rarely white; plants 1–5 ft. tall; spreading by underground stems and forming colonies. In damp, low places, meadows, stream margins, and woods. Generally distributed throughout the state and frequently cultivated in gardens.

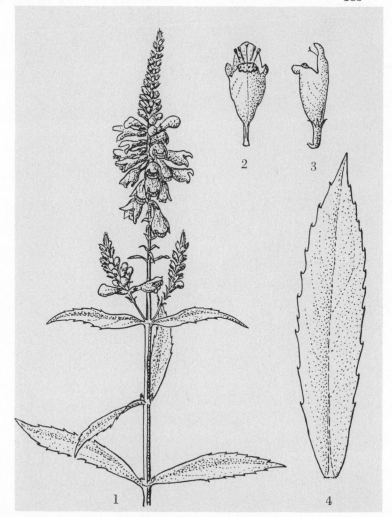

1

2

LABIATAE. Mint Family

SELFHEAL (*Prunella vulgaris*).

1. Upper part of stem, x ⅔. 2. Side and face view of corolla, x 2.

Flowers purple, blue, or violet to white; stems loosely tufted, mostly prostrate and turning up at the ends, mostly 0.2–1.0 ft. long, angled. Moist, low places in woods, shady lawns, and borders, often in disturbed soil. Generally distributed in the state except in the southwestern quarter.

LABIATAE. Mint Family

COMMON SKULLCAP (*Scutellaria epilobiifolia*).

1–2. Habit, x ½. 3. Flower in side view, x 2.
4. Mature calyx (hump behind) x 2. 5. "Seed" (i.e., ripened section of ovary, enclosing seed), x 10.

Flowers blue or lavender; stems 0.5–2.0 ft. tall, angled; spreading by means of rootstocks. Bogs, marshes, lakeshores, and wet meadows. Throughout the state.

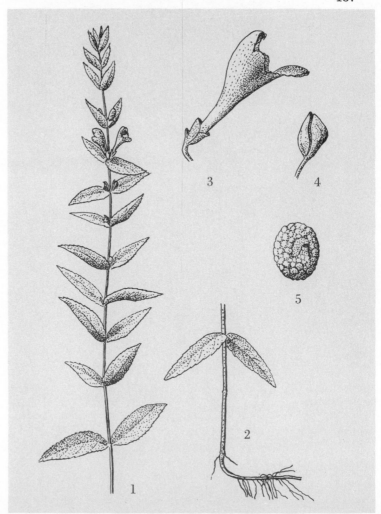

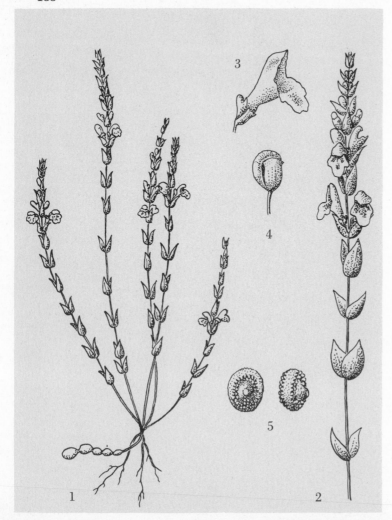

LABIATAE. Mint Family

SMALL SKULLCAP (*Scutellaria parvula*).

1. Habit, x ½. 2. Upper part of stem, x 1. 3. Side view of flower, x 2. 4. Mature calyx, x 2. 5. Basal and side views of "seed" (i.e., ripened section of ovary enclosing seed), x 10.

Flowers bluish; perennial by means of white, fleshy underground "beaded" tubers. Dry, upland prairies. Found in southern and western Minnesota south and west of a line joining Chisago, Morrison, Clay, and Polk counties.

LABIATAE. Mint Family

WOUNDWORT (*Stachys palustris*).

1. Upper part of stem, x ½. 2. Flower, x 2. 3. Stem leaf, x ½. 4. Section of stem, x 2. 5. Base of stem, x ½.

Flowers purplish, spotted or mottled with darker and lighter hues; stems 1–3 ft. tall, angled; spreading readily by underground stems. In low, wet fields, meadows, and sloughs. Throughout the state.

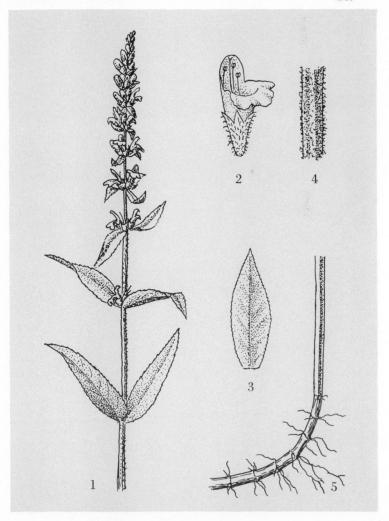

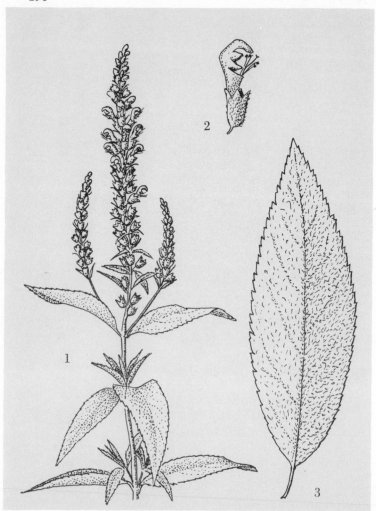

LABIATAE. *Mint Family*

AMERICAN GERMANDER (*Teucrium canadense*).

1. Upper part of stem, x ½. 2. Flower, x 2.
3. Stem leaf, x 1.

Flowers purplish to pink; stems 1–3 ft. tall, angled; spreading by underground stems. Moist to wet soil, woods, and pastures. Present in southeastern Minnesota east of a line joining Pine, Hennepin, Nicollet, and Freeborn counties; also recorded from Douglas and Mahnomen counties.

LEGUMINOSAE. *Pea or Bean Family*

HOG PEANUT (*Amphicarpa bracteata*).

1. Section of the stem, x ½. 2. Inflorescence, x 1.
3. Seed pod, x 1. 4. Underground fruit, x 1.

Flowers purple to whitish; stems slender, twining, to
3 ft. or more. In addition to the normal flowers,
others lacking petals are usually formed near the
base of the stem; these develop fruits with 1 seed
beneath the surface of the soil. Moist woods and
thickets. In the northeastern three-quarters of the
state, north and east of a line joining Blue Earth,
Morrison, and Clay counties; also reported from
Pipestone County.

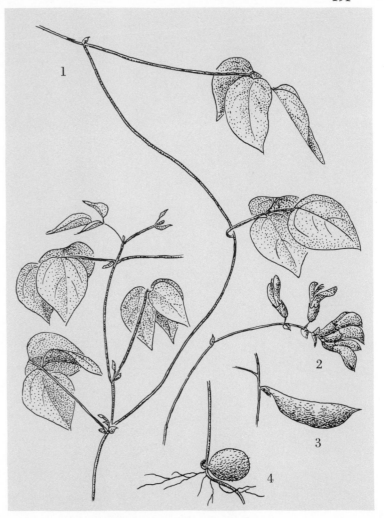

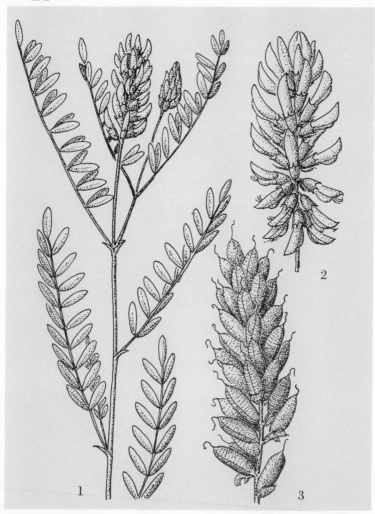

LEGUMINOSAE. Pea or Bean Family

CANADIAN MILK VETCH (*Astragalus canadensis*).

1. Upper part of stem, x ½. 2. Inflorescence, x 1.
3. Seed pods, x 1.

Flowers pale yellow or nearly white; stems 1.5–4.0
ft. tall, 1 to several from the branched crown. Open
woods and prairies. Throughout the state.

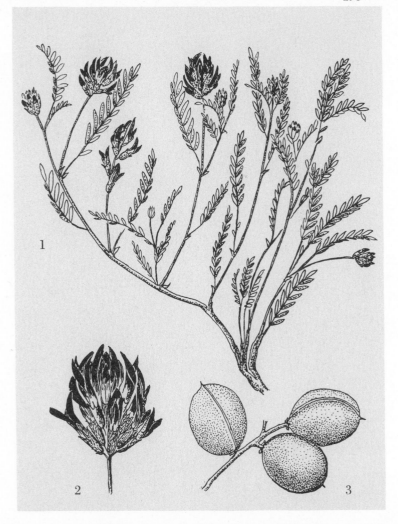

193

LEGUMINOSAE. *Pea or Bean Family*

GROUND OR PRAIRIE PLUM (*Astragalus crassicarpus*).

1. One branch from the crown, x ½. 2. Inflorescence, x 1. 3. Fruits, x 1.

Flowers bluish, purplish, or whitish. Stems usually numerous from the branched crown, reclining, with the ends turned upward; fruits plumlike, green, or purplish; the wall thick and fleshy at first, then tough and corky when ripe, not splitting open until partially decayed. Dry prairies and bluffs. Found in southern and western Minnesota south and west of a line joining Ramsey, Stearns, Mahnomen, and Kittson counties.

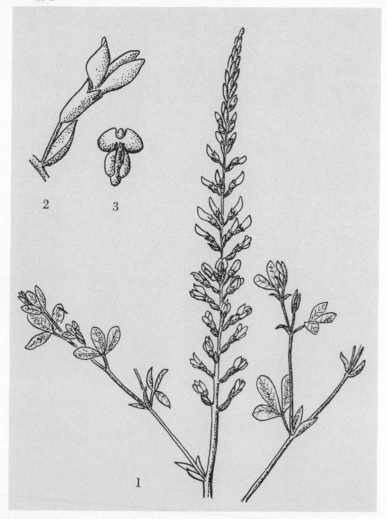

2 3

1

LEGUMINOSAE. *Pea or Bean Family*

PRAIRIE OR WHITE FALSE INDIGO (*Baptisia leucantha*).

1. Upper part of stem, x ¼. 2. Flower, x 1. 3. Face view of flower, x 1.

Flowers white. Stems 2–4 or more ft. tall, widely branched, smooth, bluish. Open woods and prairies. Southeastern Minnesota south of Hennepin and Ramsey counties and east of Faribault County. Another kind of false indigo, *B. leucophaea*, with usually cream-colored flowers and hairy stems and leaves, also occurs in southeastern Minnesota. It is found in open woods and prairies southeast of a line joining Wabasha and Steele counties.

LEGUMINOSAE. *Pea or Bean Family*

PARTRIDGE PEA; PRAIRIE SENNA (*Cassia fasciculata*).

1. Upper part of stem, x ½. 2. Flower, x 1.
3. Upper petal, x 1. 4. Seed pod, x 1.

Flowers yellow. Stems 1.0–2.5 ft. tall. Plants annual. In sandy, open, or disturbed soil. In Minnesota, south of a line joining Ramsey, Nicollet, and Chippewa counties.

1

2

3

LEGUMINOSAE. *Pea or Bean Family*

TICK-TREFOIL; TICK-CLOVER (*Desmodium canadense*).

1. Upper part of stem, x ½. 2. Flower, x 1. 3. Seed pod, x 1.

Flowers rose-purple to blue; stems 1–4 ft. tall, 1 to several from the crown; surface of the joints of the fruit covered with hooked hairs by which the fruit, when ripe, is attached to any passing animal or to an individual's clothing. The common names apply equally well to the other 4 kinds of *Desmodium* found in the state. Thickets, open woods, and banks. Throughout Minnesota except in the northeastern fifth.

LEGUMINOSAE. Pea or Bean Family

PALE VETCHLING; WILD PEA (*Lathyrus ochroleucus*).
1. Part of stem, x 1. 2. Seed pod, x 1.

Flowers yellowish-white; stems mostly 1–2 ft. high; leaves with tendrils from the tips; plants spreading by means of rootstocks. Open, moist to dry woods. Throughout Minnesota except in the southwestern corner. The other kinds of *Lathyrus* found in the state have purple or blue flowers.

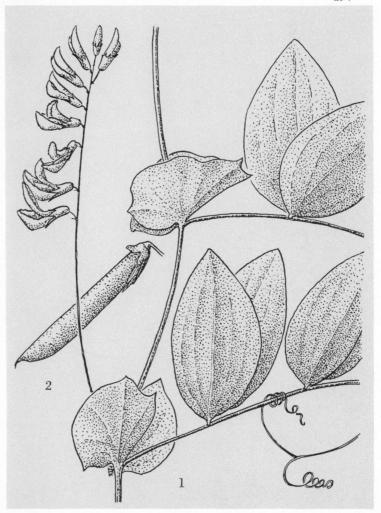

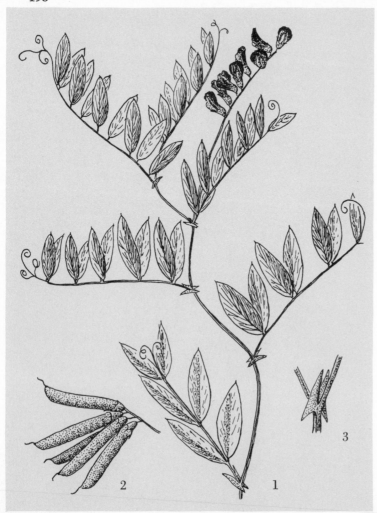

LEGUMINOSAE. *Pea or Bean Family*

VEINY VETCHLING; WILD PEA (*Lathyrus venosus*).
1. Upper portion of stem, x ½. 2. Seed pods, x ½.
3. Stipules, from the base of the leaf stalk, x 1.

Flowers purple; stems to 3–4 ft. or more long, reclining or climbing by means of tendrils; spreading by rootstocks. Moist open woods, fence rows, and thickets. Throughout the state. Another purple-flowered *Lathyrus*, *L. palustris*, sometimes referred to as the marsh vetchling, is also common throughout the state in wet meadows, marshes, and along stream courses. It is distinguished by its more narrow leaves, weaker stems, and some other more technical differences.

LEGUMINOSAE. *Pea or Bean Family*

PRAIRIE OR BIRDSFOOT-TREFOIL (*Lotus americanus*).
1. Upper part of stem, x 1. 2. Seed pod, x 1.

Flowers pink or yellowish; stems mostly a few inches
to a foot tall; plants annual. Dry prairies. Southwestern and western Minnesota; also recorded from Pine
County. Another birdsfoot trefoil, *L. corniculatus*,
a native of Europe, is now established and spreading from several points in the state. It has bright
yellow to brick-red flowers about twice as large as
the ones shown. They are borne in headlike clusters.

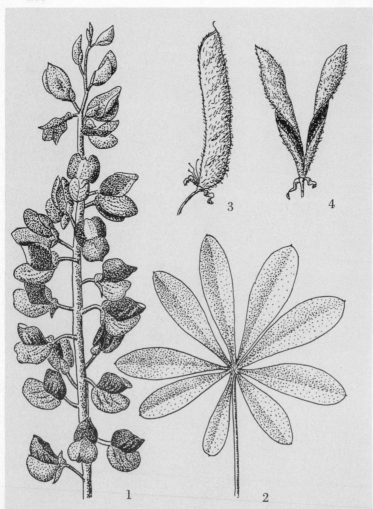

LEGUMINOSAE. *Pea or Bean Family*

WILD LUPINE (*Lupinus perennis*).

1. Inflorescence, x 1. 2. Leaf, x 1. 3. Seed pod, x 1.
4. Seed pod after seeds are shed, x 1.

Flowers blue to purple to pink or white. Stems a few inches to 1.5 ft. or more tall. Open woods, old fields, etc., usually in sandy soil. In central and southeastern Minnesota in an area bounded by a line joining southern Pine, southern Crow Wing, western Morrison, Hennepin, and Olmsted counties.

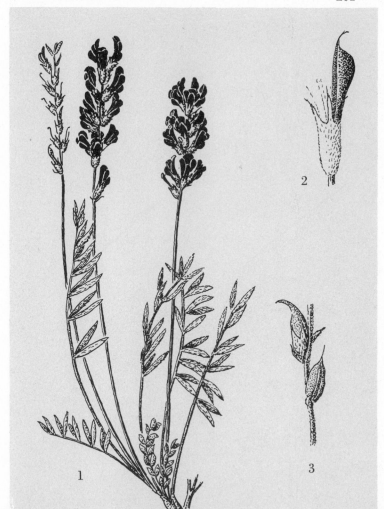

LEGUMINOSAE. *Pea or Bean Family*

LOCOWEED (*Oxytropis lambertii*).

1. A single branch from the crown, x ½. 2. Portion of flower showing beaked (pointed) keel and calyx, x 2. 3. Mature seed pods, x 1.

Flowers purple or bluish; stems 1 or more from the branched, perennial crown; both the stems and leaves either green or else silvery with silky hairs. Dry prairies. Western Minnesota from Clay County to Jackson County; also recorded from Crow Wing, Hennepin, and Ramsey counties.

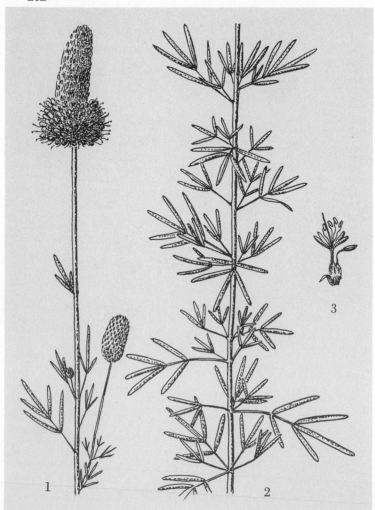

1

2

3

LEGUMINOSAE. *Pea or Bean Family*

PURPLE PRAIRIE CLOVER (*Petalostemum purpureum*).

1. Upper part of stem, x 1. 2. Middle section of stem, x 1. 3. Flower, x 2.

Flowers rose-purple; stems mostly 1.0–2.5 ft. tall, the stems and leaves lightly covered with hair. Dry hills and prairies. Throughout Minnesota, but rare in the northeastern quarter. Two other prairie clovers occur in the state. The white prairie clover, *P. candidum*, which is much like this one except that the flowers are white, has a similar distribution. The silky prairie clover, *P. villosum*, also has rose-purple flowers but the stems and leaves are densely covered with silky hair. It is found in east-central Minnesota from Morrison to Wabasha counties.

LEGUMINOSAE. *Pea or Bean Family*

SILVER-LEAVED PSORALEA; SCURF PEA (*Psoralea argophylla*).

1. Branch of stem, x 1. 2. Inflorescence, x 2.

Flowers dark blue to purple. Stems 1–2 ft. tall, widely branched, the stems and leaves ashy-gray due to the dense cover of hair. Dry prairies. Southern and western Minnesota south and west of a line joining Ramsey, Stearns, Mahnomen, and Kittson counties.

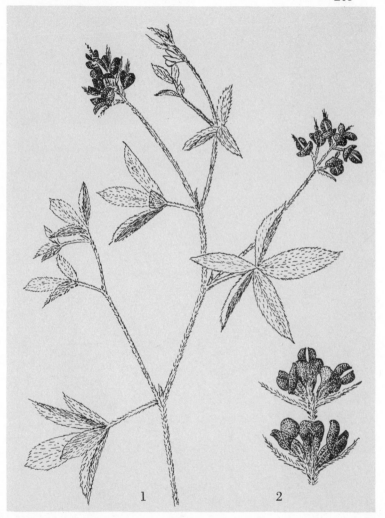

1   2

LEGUMINOSAE. Pea or Bean Family

INDIAN BREADROOT; PRAIRIE TURNIP (*Psoralea esculenta*).

1. Upper two-thirds of stem, x ½. 2. Root, x ½.

Flowers blue; stems usually a few inches to 1 ft. tall, widely branched, the stems and leaves covered with a variable amount of spreading hair; root spindle-shaped, thickened, edible. Dry prairies. Southern and western Minnesota south and west of a line joining Fillmore, Hennepin, Stearns, Mahnomen, and Kittson counties.

LEGUMINOSAE. Pea or Bean Family

WHITE CLOVER (*Trifolium repens*).

1. Outer end of stem, x 1. 2. Seed pod, x 2.

Flowers white or tinged with pink; stems prostrate, but turning upward at the ends, rooting at the nodes. In lawns, pastures, old fields, and along roadways; introduced from Europe and now fully naturalized. Throughout the state. All of the clovers of the genus *Trifolium* found in Minnesota, 7 species in all, have been introduced from Europe.

1 2

LEGUMINOSAE. *Pea or Bean Family*

AMERICAN VETCH (*Vicia americana*).

1. Outer part of stem, x 1. 2. Seed pod, x 1.

Flowers bluish-purple; stems to about 3 ft. long, weak, reclining, or climbing. Moist soil, pastures, and thickets. Found throughout the state. Two other kinds of vetch of the genus *Vicia* found in the state are introduced forage plants from Europe that sometimes escape cultivation and persist in pastures and along roadways.

LENTIBULARIACEAE. *Bladderwort Family*

BUTTERWORT (*Pinguicula vulgaris*).

1. Habit, x 1. 2. Face view of flower, x 2. 3. Capsule, x 2.

Flowers purple; stemless, all of the leaves from the crown; leaves yellowish-green. Growing in soil-filled crevices of wet rocks. North shore of Lake Superior in Lake and Cook counties.

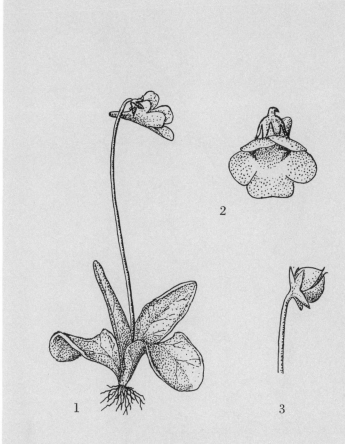

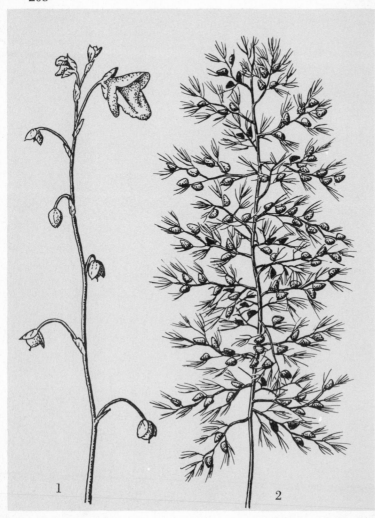

1.   2.

LENTIBULARIACEAE. Bladderwort Family

BLADDERWORT (*Utricularia vulgaris*).

1. Inflorescence, x 1. 2. Part of stem, x 1.

Flowers bright yellow; plants free floating, with the stems and leaves beneath the surface of the water and only the flowering stalks raised above the surface; leaves with numerous small bladders as shown. Quiet water of small ponds or backwaters of lakes and streams. Found throughout the state. This is the commonest and most attractive of the 5 species of bladderwort found in Minnesota.

LINACEAE. Flax Family

YELLOW FLAX (*Linum rigidum*).

1. Upper part of stem in flower, x 1. 2. Same, in fruit, x 1. 3. Capsule, x 2.

Flowers yellow; stems a few inches to a foot or more high. Prairies. Found in a broad band across the state bounded by Winona, Anoka, Brown, Yellow Medicine, Pope, and Norman counties. Another wild yellow flax, *L. sulcatum*, is also found in Minnesota. It is more common and widely distributed in the same area and also in the border counties in the west from Rock to Kittson counties; also reported from St. Louis County. The 2 flax species are distinguished by small technical characteristics of the seed pods or capsules which have 5 basal thickenings in *L. rigidum*; the thickenings are lacking in *L. sulcatum*.

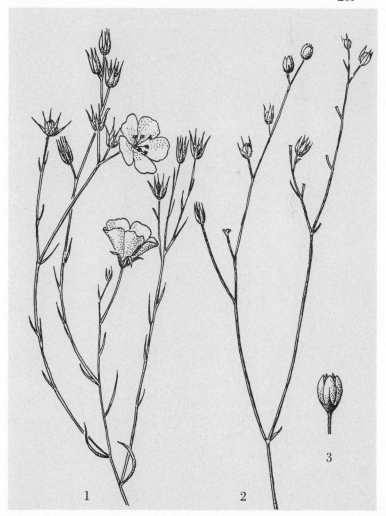

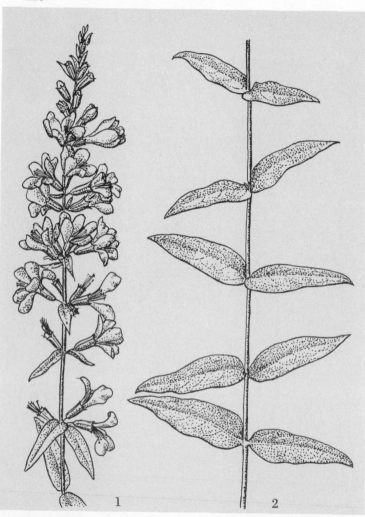

1   2

LYTHRACEAE. *Loosestrife Family*

SPIKED LOOSESTRIFE; PURPLE LOOSESTRIFE (*Lythrum salicaria*).

1. Inflorescence, x 1. 2. Middle section of stem, x 1.

Flowers reddish-purple; stems to 4 ft. or more tall, branched, 1 to several from the crown. Marshes, lakeshores, wet meadows along streams; introduced from Europe and spreading from gardens. Naturalized at scattered localities in the eastern, central, and northern parts of the state.

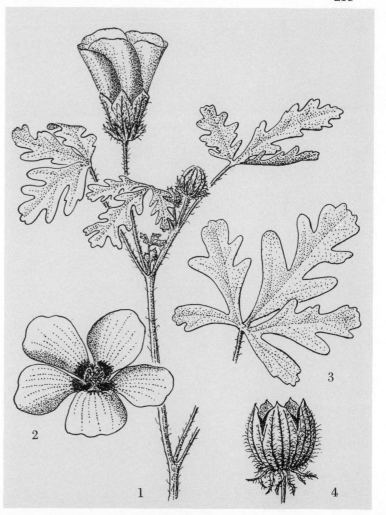

MALVACEAE. Mallow Family

FLOWER-OF-AN-HOUR (*Hibiscus trionum*).

1. Upper part of stem, x 1. 2. Flower, x 1.
3. Leaf, x 1. 4. Calyx, capsule within, x 1.

Flowers yellow; stems to about 1.5 ft. tall. Waste
ground, fields, and roadsides; introduced from
Europe. Recorded from scattered localities south
and west of a line joining Hennepin, Stearns,
and Clay counties.

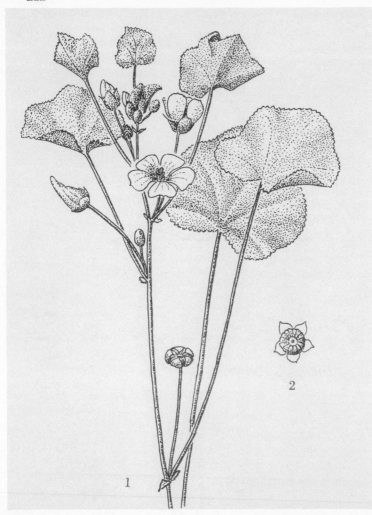

1

2

MALVACEAE. Mallow Family

COMMON MALLOW; CHEESES (*Malva neglecta*).

1. Upper part of stem, x 1. 2. Ring of carpels with a seed within each one, x 1.

Flowers pale lavender to white; stems often reclining at the base. Roadsides, old fields, etc.; introduced from Europe. Occasionally seen south of a line joining southern St. Louis, southern Hubbard, and Clay counties. Another common mallow *M. rotundifolia* is sometimes seen south and west of a line joining Ramsey, Morrison, southern Clearwater, and Kittson counties. Its differences include being less coarse, having smaller flowers, and having minor variations in certain features of the fruit.

MALVACEAE. Mallow Family

HIGH MALLOW (*Malva sylvestris*).

1. Inflorescence, x 1. 2. Leaf, x 1. 3. Ring of carpels, each enclosing a seed, x 1.

Flowers rose-purple; stems to 2 ft. or more tall, erect. Roadsides, old fields, and waste places; introduced from Europe. Southeastern Minnesota south and east of a line joining Isanti, Meeker, and Brown counties.

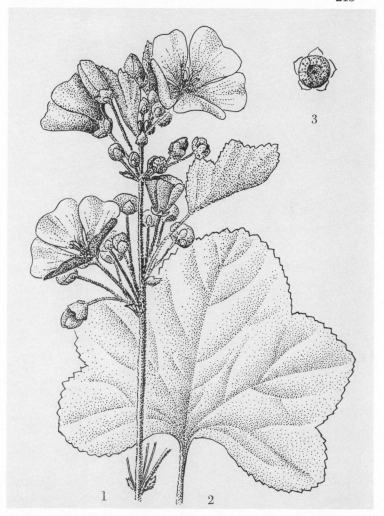

1

2

NYCTAGINACEAE. *Four-o'clock Family*

WILD FOUR-O'CLOCK; UMBRELLA-WORT (*Mirabilis nyctaginea*).

1. Habit, x $\frac{1}{10}$. 2. Upper half of stem, x 1.

Flowers (calyx) pink to purple; stems to 3 ft. or more long, from reclining to upright in position, nearly smooth, extensively branching. Prairies, often introduced into disturbed soil of fields and roadways. Found over most of the state, but commonest in the southern half; absent in the Arrowhead and adjacent counties, except where introduced in the vicinity of Duluth.

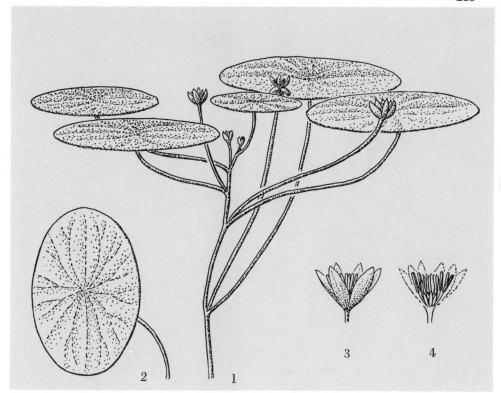

NYMPHAEACEAE. *Water Lily Family*

WATER SHIELD (*Brasenia schreberi*).

1. Upper end of stem as it floats in the water; only the flowers and upper sides of the leaves are exposed, x ½. 2. Leaf from above, x ½. 3. Side view of flower, x 1. 4. Longitudinal section of flower, x 1.

Flowers dull purple; stems trailing through the water; leaves floating on the surface; all of the underwater surfaces covered with a thick, transparent, gelatinous layer. Shallow water of quiet ponds and backwaters of lakes. In eastern and northeastern Minnesota north and east of a line joining Le Sueur, Otter Tail, Clearwater, and Itasca counties.

216

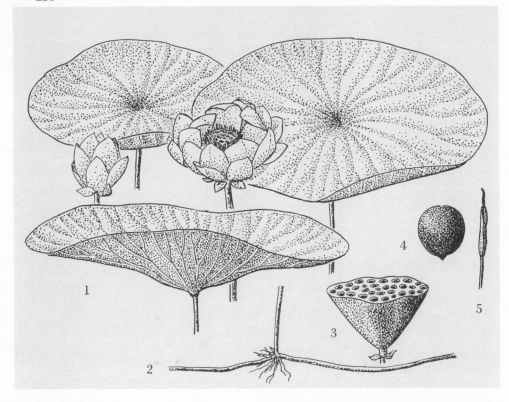

NYMPHAEACEAE. Water Lily Family

AMERICAN LOTUS LILY;
YELLOW NELUMBO; WATER
CHINQUAPIN (*Nelumbo lutea*).

1. Flowers and leaves as they appear above the water, x ¼. 2. Rootstock, x ¼. 3. Fruiting receptacle, x ¼. 4. Fruit, x 1. 5. Stamen, x 1.

Flowers pale yellow, on long stalks or peduncles rising as much as 3 ft. above the water; shieldlike leaves also usually raised high above the water on their stalks; both nutlike fruits and tubers edible. Quiet backwaters of rivers and bays; ponds. Found in the Twin Cities area (Lake Minnetonka; lower Minnesota River Valley) and along the Mississippi River to Houston County.

NYMPHAEACEAE. *Water Lily Family*

YELLOW WATER LILY; POND LILY (*Nuphar variegatum*).

1. Leaf, x ½. 2. Flower, x ½. 3. Rhizome, x ½.
4. Ripened ovary with seeds within, x ½. 5. Sepals,
x 1. 6. Petals, x 1. 7. Stamen, x 1. 8. Young ovary, x 1.

Flowers yellow, the sepals leathery; the inside of the inner three sepals tending to be suffused with red toward the base; the exposed outer surfaces of the sepals (in the bud) green; leaf blades floating on the surface; stem (rhizome) 1–3 in. or more thick, embedded in and rooted to the bottom. In ponds, quiet water of protected bays, etc. Found over most of the state, but uncommon or absent in most of the prairie areas to the west. The small yellow pond lily, *N. microphyllum*, also occurs in Minnesota in some abundance in the Arrowhead region, Cook, Lake, and St. Louis counties.

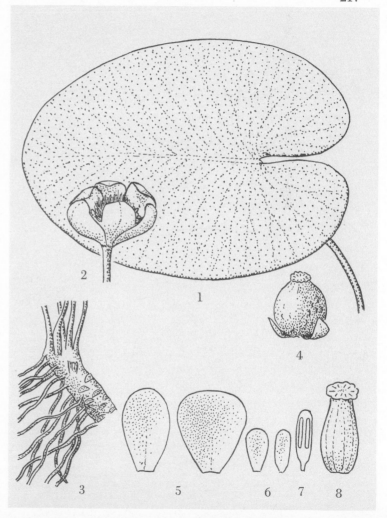

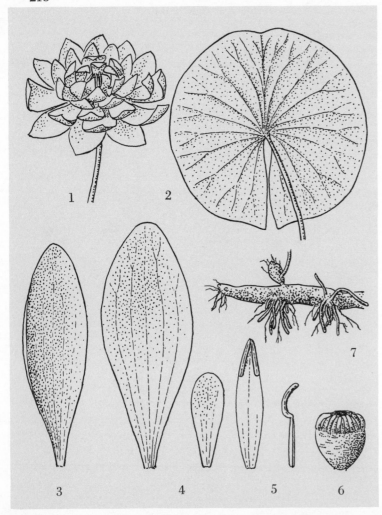

NYMPHAEACEAE. *Water Lily Family*

WHITE WATER LILY (*Nymphaea tuberosa*).

1. Flower, x ¼. 2. Leaf, x ¼. 3. Sepal, x 1. 4. Petals, x 1. 5. Staminode and stamen, x 1. 6. Young ovary, x 1. 7. Rhizome, x ¼.

Flowers white or pinkish, the sepals 4, the petals numerous, in a graded series; leaf blades floating on the surface; branched stem (rhizome) buried in and rooted to the bottom, producing numerous tubers along its sides. Ponds, bays, and quiet backwaters. North and east of a line joining Freeborn, Nicollet, Otter Tail, Clearwater, and northern St. Louis counties; also recorded from Pipestone County. The fragrant water lily, *N. odorata*, a very similar species, is reported over much the same range in Minnesota, but is less common.

ONAGRACEAE. *Evening Primrose Family*

ENCHANTER'S NIGHTSHADE (*Circaea quadrisulcata*).

1. Inflorescence in fruit and flower, x 1. 2. Upper part of stem, x ¼.

Parts of flowers in twos; petals whitish or pinkish; stems 0.5–2.5 ft. tall; plants spreading by rootstocks. Moist woods in organic soil. Widely distributed but rare in the northeastern quarter and not recorded from the northwestern and southwestern corners. Two more species of enchanter's nightshade occur in Minnesota. The more important one, *C. alpina*, is smaller and has more delicate, pale-green leaves. It has a similar distribution except that it is most common in the northeastern quarter.

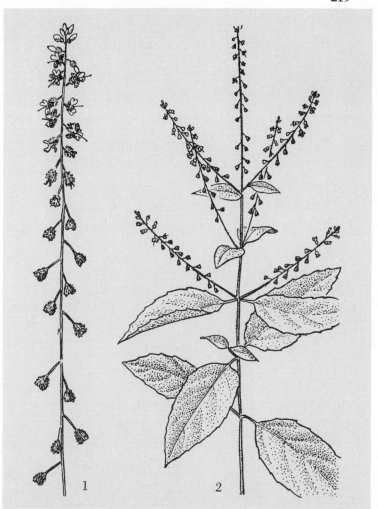

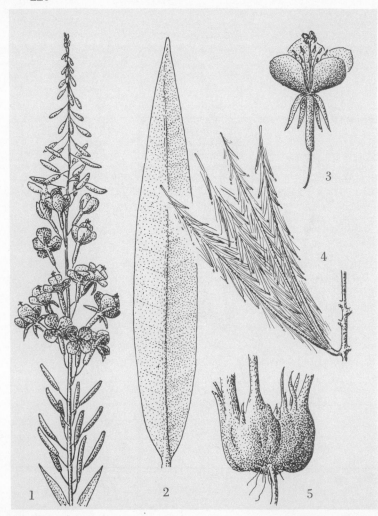

1 2 3 4 5

ONAGRACEAE. *Evening Primrose Family*

FIREWEED; GREAT WILLOW-HERB (*Epilobium angustifolium*).

1. Inflorescence in fruit and flower, x ½. 2. Stem leaf, x 1. 3. Flower, x 1. 4. Opened seed pod, x 1. 5. Base of plant and underground parts, x 1.

Flowers pink-purple, rarely white; stems mostly 1–4 ft. tall. Margins of woods, forest openings, old burns, and moist to dry, often disturbed, soil. Widespread north and east of a line joining Winona, Scott, Pope, Polk, and Kittson counties. This is the most conspicuous and attractive of several kinds of willow-herb that occur in the state.

ONAGRACEAE. *Evening Primrose Family*

SCARLET GAURA (*Gaura coccinea*).

1. One stem from the base, x ½. 2. Upper half of a branch, x 1. 3. Mature seed pods, still attached, x 4.

Petals reddish-pink to white; stems 1 to several from the perennial crown, more or less reclining at the base, both the stems and leaves grayish-green. Dry prairies. Found in the border and adjacent counties in the western quarter of the state.

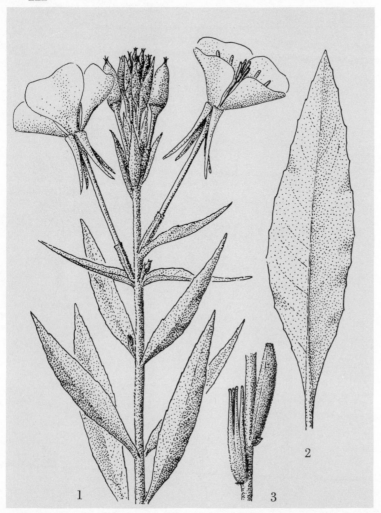

1

3

2

ONAGRACEAE. Evening Primrose Family

EVENING PRIMROSE (*Oenothera biennis*).

1. Upper part of stem, x 1. 2. Stem leaf, x 1. 3. Mature seed pods, still attached, x 1.

Petals yellow; stems 1–5 ft. or more tall; plants biennial. Old fields, roadsides, and prairies. Recorded from eastern and central Minnesota east of a line joining Lake of the Woods, Beltrami, Pope, Chippewa, and Waseca counties. The common name applies equally well to several other species of the genus *Oenothera* found in the state.

ONAGRACEAE. Evening Primrose Family

EVENING PRIMROSE (*Oenothera rhombipetala*).

1. Upper part of stem, x 1. 2. Young seed pod, x 1.
3. Stem leaf, x 1.

Petals yellow; stems 1–3 ft. tall, extensively branching; plants biennial. Sandy prairies, especially in the Anoka Sand Plain. Found in southeastern Minnesota east of a line joining Anoka, Hennepin, Dakota, Olmsted, and Houston counties.

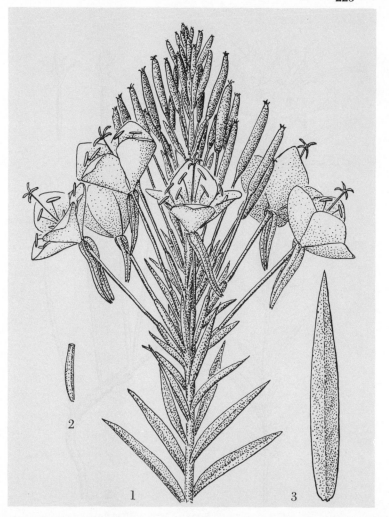

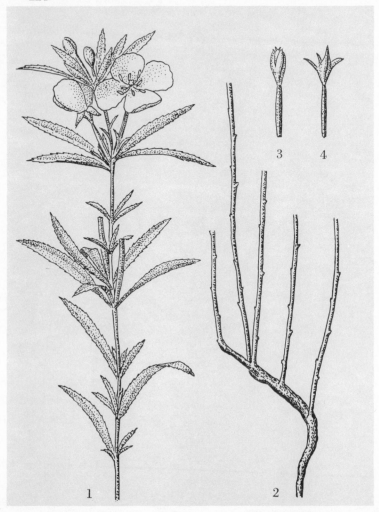

1
2
3   4

ONAGRACEAE. *Evening Primrose Family*

TOOTH-LEAVED EVENING PRIMROSE (*Oenothera serrulata*).

1. Upper part of stem, x 1. 2. Lower part of stem, x 1. 3. Opening bud, x 1. 4. Calyx and ovary of opening bud (petals removed), x 1.

Petals yellow; stems 0.5–1.5 ft. long, semiwoody below, 1 to several stems from the crown, often partially reclining at the base; leaves with fine teeth along the edges; plants perennial. Dry prairies. Southern and western Minnesota south and west of a line joining Ramsey, Morrison, and Kittson counties.

OXALIDACEAE. Wood Sorrel Family

WOOD SORREL; SHEEP SORREL (*Oxalis stricta*).

1. Upper half of stem, x 1. 2. Mature seed pods, x 1. 3. Root, x 1.

Petals yellow; stems to 1 ft. or more high; plants spreading by underground stems; herbage very sour tasting. Disturbed, moist soil around shrubbery along wood roads, field margins, etc.; sometimes weedy. Recorded from most parts of the state except the north-central counties; very common in the southern half.

WOOD SORREL (*Oxalis dillenii*).

4. Mature seed pods, x 1.

Very similar, but shorter, lacking the underground stems; the seed pods with bent stalks, as shown. Frequent in southern Minnesota, but rare or absent in the north.

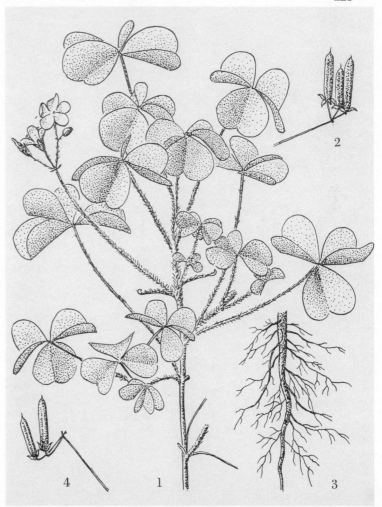

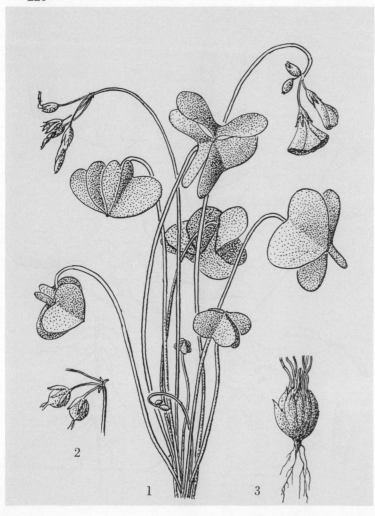

2

1   3

OXALIDACEAE. *Wood Sorrel Family*

VIOLET WOOD SORREL (*Oxalis violacea*).

1. Plant to ground level, x 1. 2. Mature seed pods, x 1. 3. Underground parts, x 1.

Petals pinkish-violet to white. Open woods and prairies. Recorded from south and west of a line joining Chisago, Morrison, and Polk counties.

PAPAVERACEAE. *Poppy Family*

BLOODROOT *(Sanguinaria canadensis)*.

1. Above-ground parts, x 1. 2. Seed pod, x 1.

Petals white or rarely pink; spreading vigorously from thick, partially buried, horizontal stems with orange-red sap. Rich, moist woods, often in full shade after the trees are leafed out in the spring. In almost all of the wooded parts of the state, but commonest in the central and southeastern counties.

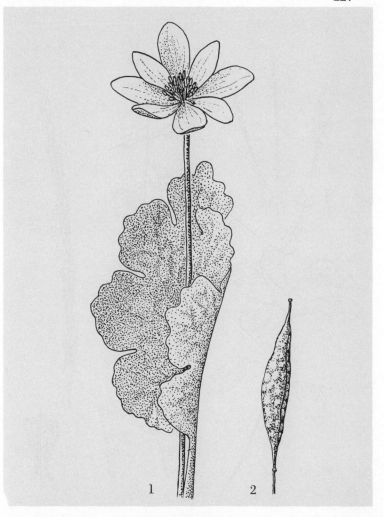

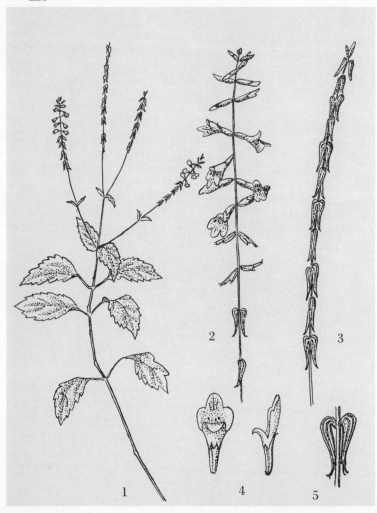

1

2

3

4

5

PHRYMACEAE. Lopseed Family

LOPSEED (*Phryma leptostachya*).

1. Upper part of stem, x ⅕. 2. Branch of inflorescence, x 1. 3. Branch of inflorescence with developing seed pods, x 1. 4. Face and side view of flower, x 2. 5. Two mature seed pods still attached, x 2.

Petals purplish to rose to whitish; stems mostly 1.0–2.5 ft. tall. Moist thickets and woods. Widely distributed in wooded parts of the state; not reported from the northeastern, northwestern, and southwestern corners.

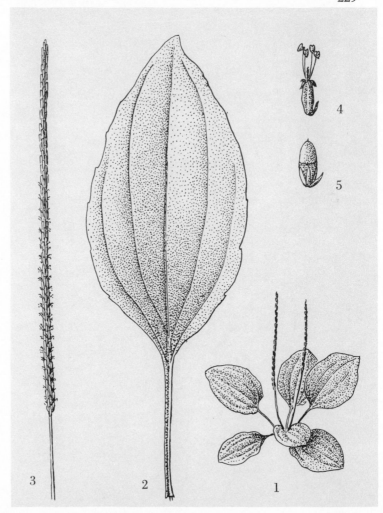

PLANTAGINACEAE. *Plantain Family*

COMMON PLANTAIN (*Plantago major*).

1. Habit, x ⅛. 2. Leaf, x ½. 3. Inflorescence, x ½.
4. Flower, x 3. 5. Mature seed pod, x 3.

Corolla greenish or whitish. Common in moist soil,
in full sun or partial shade; introduced from Europe.
There are a large number of native and introduced
plantains in Minnesota, but this is the commonest
and best known. Found throughout the state.

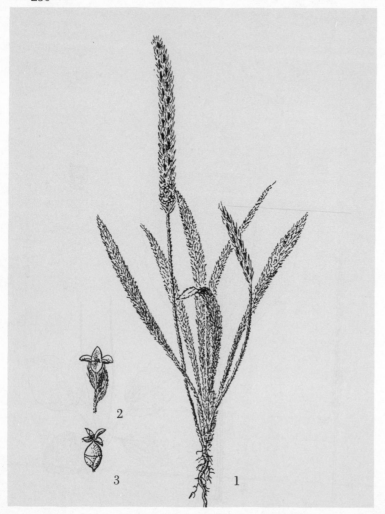

1

2

3

PLANTAGINACEAE. Plantain Family

PLANTAIN (*Plantago purshii*).

1. Habit, x ¾. 2. Flower, x 3. 3. Mature seed pod and remnants of the corolla adhering to the tip, x 3.

Corolla whitish; stems and leaves silvery with silky hairs; annual. Dry roadsides and sterile fields; varying greatly in size in response to available moisture; native, but often weedy. In Minnesota, south and west of a line joining Washington, Morrison, and Becker counties; also recorded from southern St. Louis and Cook counties and to be expected elsewhere.

POLEMONIACEAE. *Phlox Family*

WILD BLUE PHLOX (*Phlox divaricata*).

1–2. Habit, x 1. 3. Mature seed pods still attached, x 1.

Corolla blue to purplish or white; stems mostly 0.5–
1.5 ft. tall, the base often reclining; gradually spreads
by means of prostrate basal branches. Rich, moist
woods and margins. In southern Minnesota south of
a line joining southern Pine, Meeker, and Lac
Qui Parle counties.

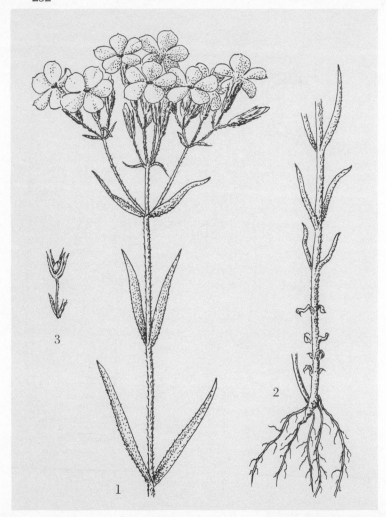

3

1

2

POLEMONIACEAE. *Phlox Family*

PRAIRIE PHLOX; DOWNY PHLOX (*Phlox pilosa*).
1–2. Habit, x 1. 3. Mature seed pod still attached, x 1.

Corolla rose to violet; stems mostly 0.5–1.5 ft. tall;
nonflowering basal shoots upright or turned upward;
all parts, especially the stem, covered with soft hair
to a greater or lesser extent. Open woods and prairies. Found in the southern two-thirds of the state,
south of a line joining Pine, southern Cass, Hubbard, and Mahnomen counties.

POLEMONIACEAE. *Phlox Family*

JACOB'S LADDER (*Polemonium reptans*).

1. Upper part of stem, x 1. 2. Leaf, x 1.

Corolla pale to darker blue; stems mostly 0.5–1.5 ft. tall, often many together in a loose tuft, sometimes single or a few together. Rich woods and bottom lands. In southeastern Minnesota, north and west to Ramsey, Scott, and Mower counties.

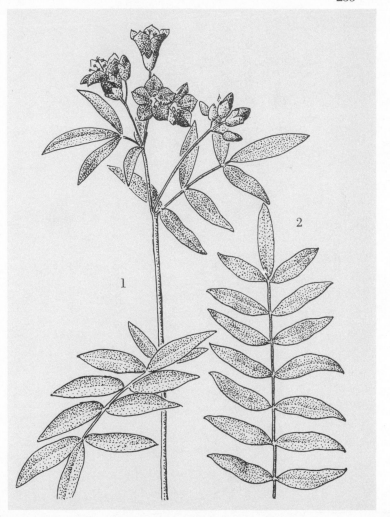

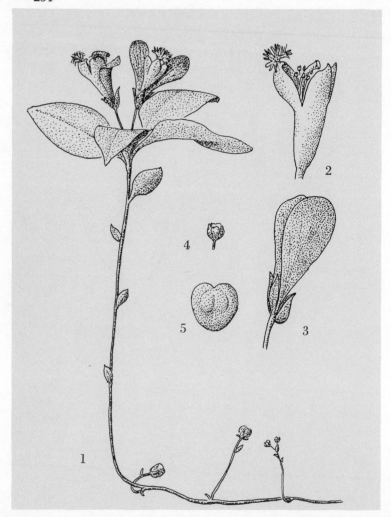

POLYGALACEAE. *Milkwort Family*

FLOWERING WINTERGREEN; FRINGED POLYGALA (*Polygala paucifolia*).

1. Habit, x 1. 2. Flower with calyx removed, x 2. 3. Calyx, x 2. 4. Cleistogamous flower, x 2. 5. Fruit, x 2.

Flowers rose-purple to white. Moist to dry woods, often in sandy soil. Found in northeastern Minnesota west to Beltrami and Hubbard counties and south to northern Anoka County.

POLYGALACEAE. *Milkwort Family*

PURPLE MILKWORT (*Polygala sanguinea*).

1. Upper half of flowering stem, x 1. 2. Upper half of fruiting stem, x 1. 3. Fruit plus remnants of floral envelope, x 4.

Flowers rose-purple to white or greenish; stems mostly 0.5–1.0 ft. tall; plants annual. Old fields, meadows, and open woods, often in sandy soil. Southeastern Minnesota west to Blue Earth and north to Stearns, Crow Wing, and Chisago counties.

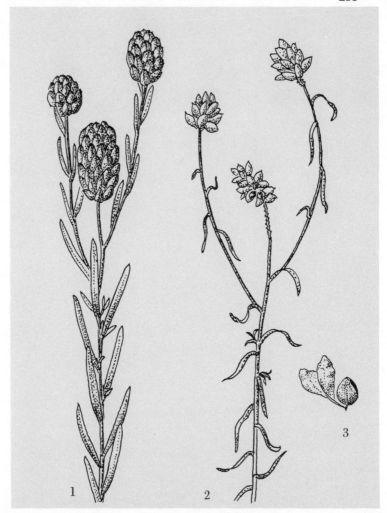

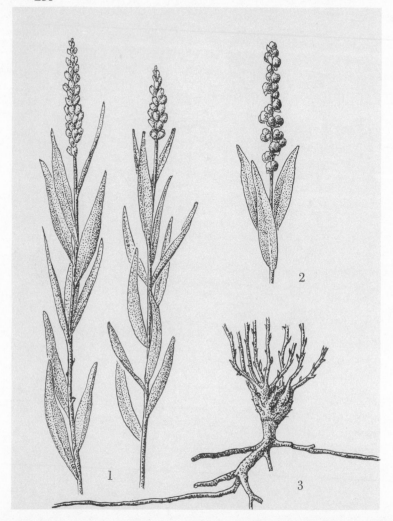

1

2

3

POLYGALACEAE. *Milkwort Family*

SENECA SNAKEROOT (*Polygala senega*).

1. Upper part of 2 stems, x 1. 2. Upper part of stem in fruit, x 1. 3. Base of plant showing perennial crown and roots, x 1.

Flowers white; stems 0.5–1.5 ft. tall, 1 to several from a branched crown; perennial, the taproot thick. Moist, open woods and prairies. Southeastern, central, and northwestern Minnesota; not recorded from the Arrowhead and adjacent counties or from the southwestern corner.

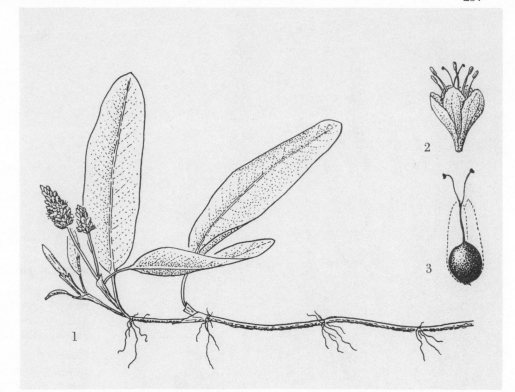

*POLYGONACEAE. Buck-
wheat Family*

WATER SMARTWEED (*Polygonum
amphibium*).

1. Habit of aquatic form, x ½.
2. Flower, x 4. 3. Fruit, x 4.

Flowers pink or rose; flower clusters 1–4 times longer than broad;
stems either trailing through the
water with the leaves floating and both the stems and leaves completely smooth,
or the stems spreading to the adjacent wet banks, more or less upright and either
smooth or hairy. Found in quiet, shallow ponds and backwaters throughout the state.

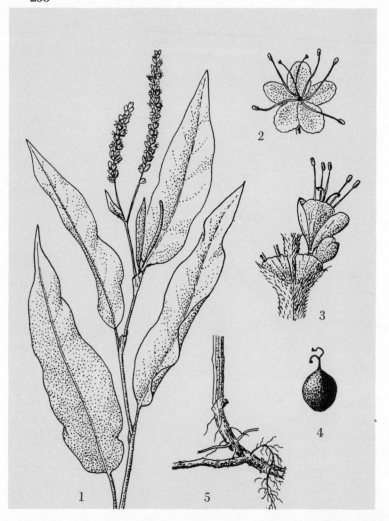

POLYGONACEAE. *Buckwheat Family*

SWAMP SMARTWEED (*Polygonum coccineum*).

1. Upper part of stem of terrestrial form, x ½. 2. Face view of flower, x 4. 3. Side views of flowers, x 4. 4. Ovary containing a single seed, x 4. 5. Prostrate base of stem and adventitious roots, x ½.

Flowers pink or rose, rarely white. Aquatic forms very similar to the water smartweed, the flower clusters 4–10 times longer than broad; more commonly seen along shores, in shallow water, or in ephemeral puddles along drainage ditches, the stems at least partially erect and covered with somewhat rough hair. Throughout the state.

POLYGONACEAE. *Buckwheat Family*

PINKWEED; SMARTWEED (*Polygonum pensylvanicum*).

1. Upper part of stem, x ½. 2. Face view of flower, x 4. 3. Side view of bud and flower, x 4. 4. Ovary containing a single seed, x 4. 5. Base of stem and root system, x ½.

Flowers pink to white; stems to 4 ft. or more tall, often widely branched; plants annual. Wet to moist places, fields, roadways, and shores. Present in most parts of the state, but commonest in the southern half. There are 25 or more kinds of smartweeds and knotweeds of the genus *Polygonum* in Minnesota.

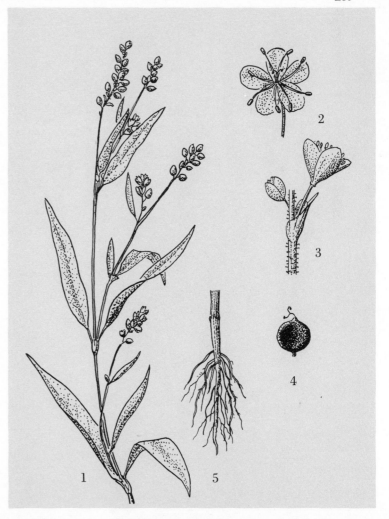

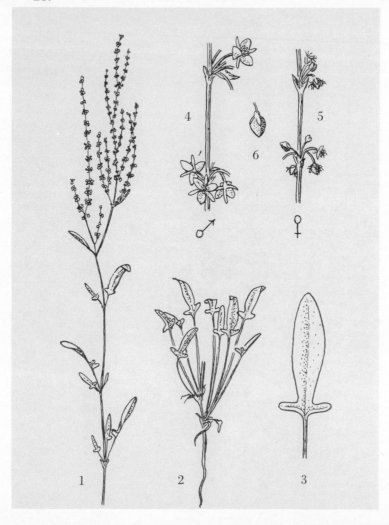

POLYGONACEAE. *Buckwheat Family*

SHEEP SORREL; COMMON RED SORREL (*Rumex acetosella*).

1–2. Habit, x ½. 3. Basal leaf, x 1. 4. Section of staminate inflorescence, x 4. 5. Section of pistillate inflorescence, x 4. 6. Ovary containing a single seed, x 4.

Flowers reddish or yellowish; stems mostly 0.5–1.5 ft. tall; the herbage tending to be reddish or purplish, especially under dry conditions; plants of 2 kinds, staminate and pistillate, spreading by slender rootstocks and forming patches or colonies. Dry pastures, fields, and roadways, in soils of low fertility; introduced from Europe. Frequently seen in the eastern half of the state; recorded from a few isolated localities in the west.

POLYGONACEAE. *Buckwheat Family*

YELLOW OR SOUR DOCK (*Rumex crispus*).

1. Inflorescence in young fruit, x ½. 2. Basal stem leaf, x ½. 3. Side view of flower, x 4. 4. Young ovary, with the floral envelope removed, x 4. 5. Mature fruits showing tubercle on back of valve, x 4. 6. Joint of stem, x ½.

Flowers greenish or purplish; stems to 3 ft. or more tall; each of the 3 valves of the fruit usually with a swelling or tubercle on the back; margins of the leaves definitely crinkled. Moist to wet places in fields, pastures, and along roadways; introduced from Europe. Present throughout the state. Several other kinds of dock, both introduced and native, are found in our area.

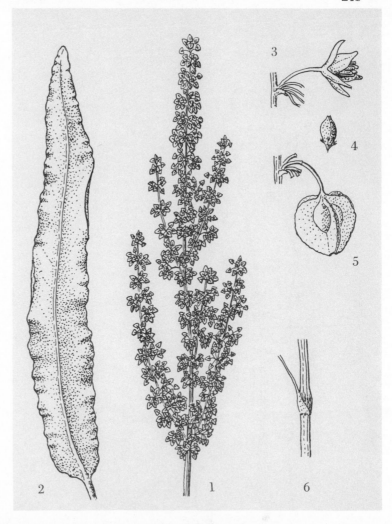

242

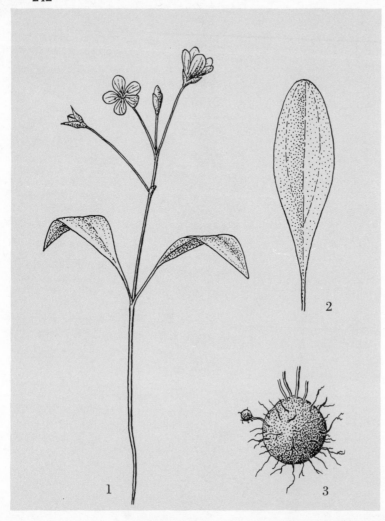

2

1

3

PORTULACACEAE. Purslane Family

SPRING BEAUTY (*Claytonia caroliniana*).

1. Flowering stem, x 1. 2. Single leaf from corm, x 1. 3. Corm, x 1.

Petals white or pink with darker stripes; stems and leaves succulent; blades of stem leaves about 2.5–4.5 times as long as wide; corms remaining in the soil when the stems are pulled. Rich, low woods. Known for certain only from St. Louis County.

PORTULACACEAE. *Purslane Family*

SPRING BEAUTY (*Claytonia virginica*).

1. Flowering stem, x 1. 2. Corm, x 1.

Like *C. caroliniana* but the blades of the stem leaves 5–15 times as long as wide. Rich, moist woods and alluvial bottoms. This is our common spring beauty found over large areas of the state south and east of a line joining southern St. Louis, Morrison, Blue Earth, and Mower counties.

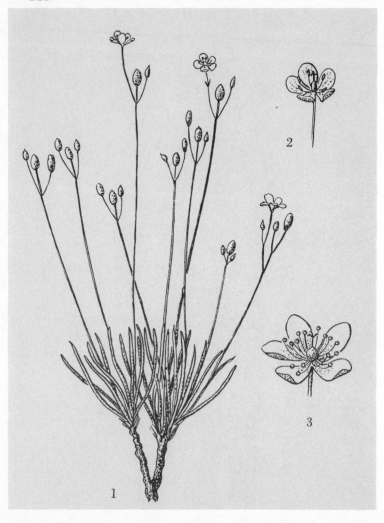

1

2

3

PORTULACACEAE. *Purslane Family*

TALINUM; FAMEFLOWER (*Talinum parviflorum*).
1. Habit, x 1. 2. Flower, x 2.

Petals white or pale pink, open for only a few hours
on sunny days; stamens 4–8 (usually 5); herbage
succulent. In thin, sterile soil, rocky outcrops, etc.
Present in the southwestern quarter of the state,
bounded by a line connecting Blue Earth, Benton,
and Big Stone counties.

TALINUM; FAMEFLOWER (*Talinum rugospermum*).
3. Flower, x 2.

Very similar but the flowers somewhat larger, the
petals pink, and the stamens 10–25 in number.
Known from Chisago, Goodhue, and Winona
counties.

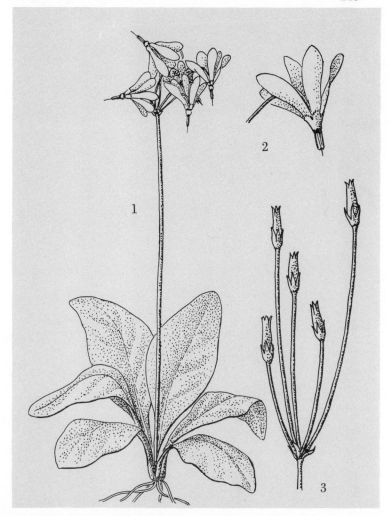

PRIMULACEAE. Primrose Family

SHOOTING STAR (*Dodecatheon radicatum*).

1. Habit, x ½. 2. Flower, x 1. 3. Inflorescence with mature capsules, x 1.

Corolla deep rose-purple, rarely white. Moist, wooded bluffs, and ledges. In the southeastern corner of the state: Wabasha, Winona, Houston, and Fillmore counties. One of our most exotic and captivating wild flowers.

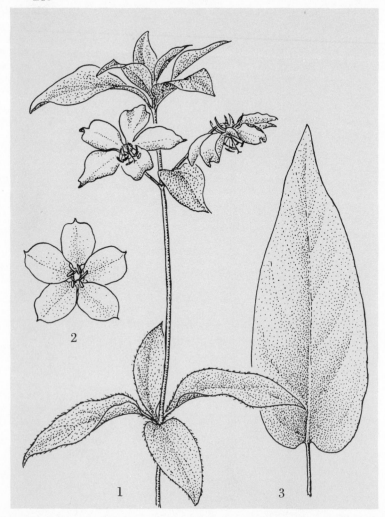

1

2

3

PRIMULACEAE. *Primrose Family*

FRINGED LOOSESTRIFE (*Lysimachia ciliata*).

1. Upper part of plant, x 1. 2. Face view of flower, x 1. 3. Middle stem leaf, x ½.

Corolla yellow; stems 0.5–3.0 ft. tall, arising from a slender, underground rootstock. In low, wet woods, marshes, and lakeshores. Present throughout the state.

PRIMULACEAE. *Primrose Family*

TUFTED LOOSESTRIFE (*Lysimachia thyrsiflora*).

1. Upper part of stem, x ½. 2. Flower, x 2. 3. Mature capsule, x 2. 4. Inflorescence in fruit, x 1. 5. Stem leaf, x 1.

Corolla yellow marked with darker spots; stems 0.5–2.5 ft. tall, arising from creeping rootstocks, smooth. Wet meadows, marshes, and swamps. Found throughout the state.

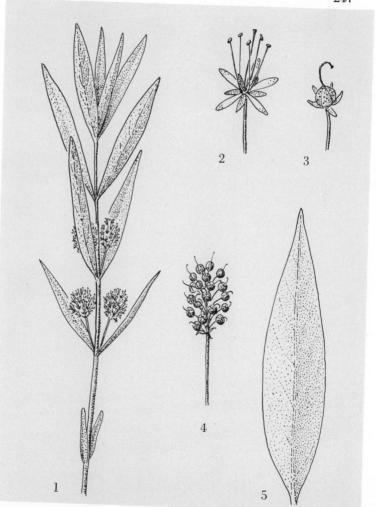

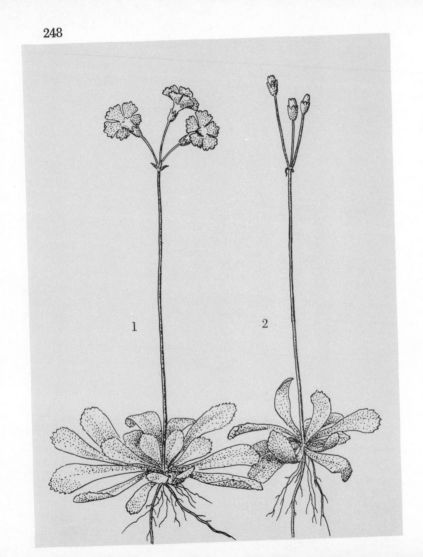

1   2

PRIMULACEAE. *Primrose Family*

MISTASSINI PRIMROSE (*Primula mistassinica*).

1. Habit of flowering plant, x 1. 2. Habit of plant with mature capsules, x 1.

Corolla lilac, pink, or bluish-purple, rarely white; under surfaces of the leaves sometimes coated with a yellowish, mealy powder. Rock crevices and depressions along the north shore of Lake Superior and similar habitats along rivers in Pine and Washington counties; also reported from Norman County.

PRIMULACEAE. *Primrose Family*

STARFLOWER (*Trientalis borealis*).

1. Habit, x ½. 2. Leaf, x 1. 3. Face view of flower, x 1. 4. Rear view of flower, x 1. 5. Capsule, x 1.

Flowers white. In moist woods and at edges of bogs. In the northeastern three-fifths of the state, north and east of a line joining Goodhue, Wright, Otter Tail, and Kittson counties.

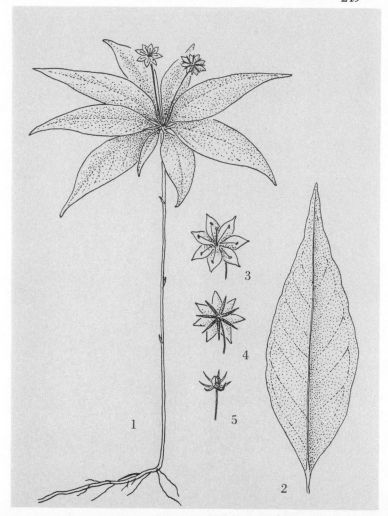

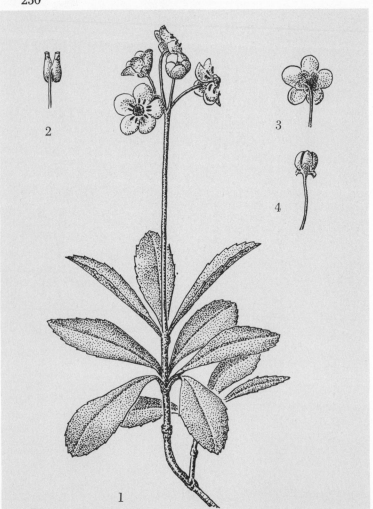

1

2

3

4

PYROLACEAE. Shinleaf Family

PIPSISSEWA; PRINCE'S PINE (*Chimaphila umbellata*).

1. Habit, x 1. 2. Anther, x 4. 3. Rear view of flower, x 1. 4. Mature capsule, x 1.

Corolla whitish-pink; stems spreading; leaves thick and leathery. Dry woods, often in sandy soil. Present north and east of a line joining Fillmore, Stearns, Clearwater, and Roseau counties.

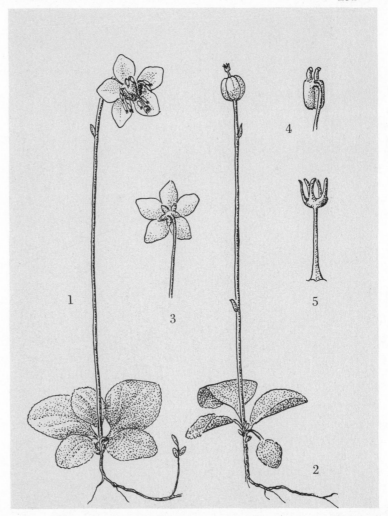

PYROLACEAE. *Shinleaf Family*

ONE-FLOWERED PYROLA (*Moneses uniflora*).

1. Habit in flower, x 1. 2. Habit in fruit, x 1. 3. Rear view of flower, x 1. 4. Anther, x 4. 5. Stigma and style, x 4.

Corolla white or tinged with pink, fragrant. Damp, mossy woods and bogs. Northeastern Minnesota west to eastern Otter Tail and eastern Mahnomen counties.

1   2

PYROLACEAE. *Shinleaf Family*

INDIAN PIPE (*Monotropa uniflora*).

1. Flowering stem, x 1. 2. Stem in fruit, x 1.

Entire plant waxy-white or sometimes pinkish; stems solitary or more often in a clump, fleshy. In deep humus, moist woods. Distributed east of a line joining Fillmore, Rice, Stearns, Clearwater, and Koochiching counties.

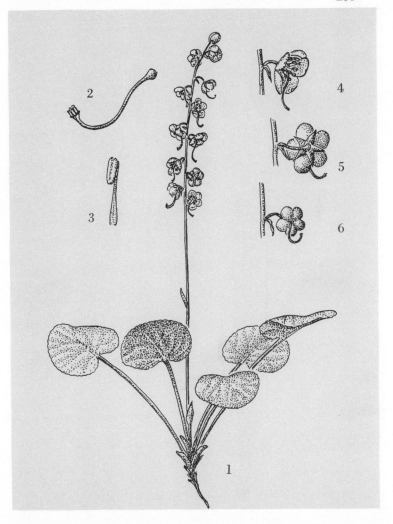

PYROLACEAE. *Shinleaf Family*

PINK-FLOWERED PYROLA; WINTERGREEN; SHINLEAF
(*Pyrola asarifolia*).

1. Habit, x ½. 2. Stigma and style, x 3. 3. Stamen, x
3. 4. Side view of flower, x 1. 5. Rear view of flower,
x 1. 6. Mature capsule, x 1.

Corolla pink to pale purple; stems creeping extensively; leaves leathery, shiny. Low, wet woods and
bogs. Central, northern, and northeastern Minnesota,
north and east of a line joining Dakota, Pope,
Becker, and Kittson counties. This is the commonest
and possibly the most attractive of our 6 species
of *Pyrola*.

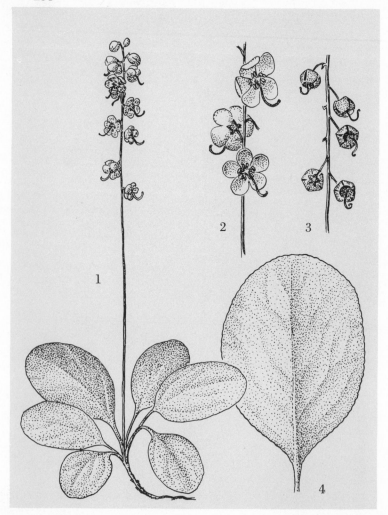

PYROLACEAE. Shinleaf Family

COMMON PYROLA; SHINLEAF (*Pyrola elliptica*).

1. Habit, x ½. 2. Part of inflorescence in flower, x 1.
3. Part of inflorescence in fruit, x 1. 4. Leaf, x 1.

Corolla white; stems spreading just beneath the surface; leaves rather thin, pale green. Dry, upland woods. In the eastern half of the state west to Waseca, Kandiyohi, Becker, and Kittson counties.

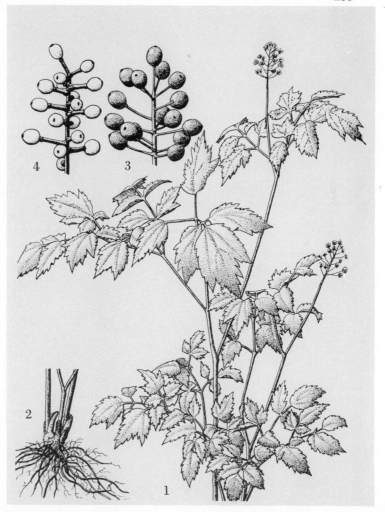

RANUNCULACEAE. *Buttercup or Crowfoot Family*

RED BANEBERRY (*Actaea rubra*).

1–2. Habit, x ¼. 3. Berries, x ¾.

Flower clusters white; stems 1.0–2.5 ft. tall, 1 to several from the crown; berries cherry-red or less commonly white, lustrous; poisonous. Rich, moist woodlands. Found throughout the state.

WHITE BANEBERRY (*Actaea pachypoda*).

4. Berries, x ¾.

Very similar, but the berries generally white, rarely red, and their stalks very stout. Southern Lake, southern St. Louis, Carlton, and Hennepin counties.

2   1

RANUNCULACEAE. *Buttercup or Crowfoot Family*

CANADA ANEMONE (*Anemone canadensis*).

1. Upper part of stem, x 1. 2. Cluster of achenes from single flower, x 1.

Flowers white; stems mostly 1–2 ft. tall; plants spreading readily by underground rootstocks and often forming large colonies. Damp, low ground in meadows, prairies, and woods. Found throughout the state. This is the most common and conspicuous of our 8 kinds of wild *Anemone*.

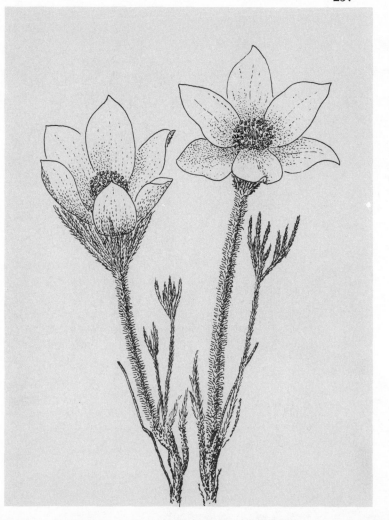

RANUNCULACEAE. Buttercup or Crowfoot Family

PASQUE·FLOWER (*Anemone patens*).

Upper part of plant, x 1.

Flowers varying from blue to purple or white; stems 0.4–1.0 ft. tall, one or more from the branched, perennial crown; stems and leaves grayish because of the covering of long, silky hair; deep-rooted. Dry prairies, hillsides, and sand plains. South and west of a line joining Washington, Crow Wing, and Roseau counties. A favorite early spring flower.

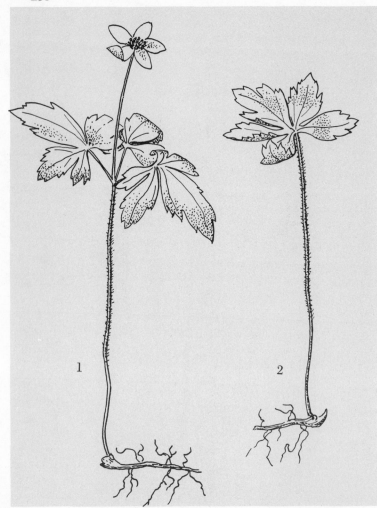

1

2

RANUNCULACEAE. Buttercup or Crowfoot Family

WOOD ANEMONE (*Anemone quinquefolia*).

1. Habit, x ⅔. 2. Young plant from rhizome, x ⅔.

Flowers white, sometimes pinkish or purplish underneath; flowering stems 1 at a place; spreading by slender, underground rootstocks. Moist, open woods and thickets. Found in central and eastern Minnesota; rare or absent from most parts of the northwestern and southwestern quarters.

RANUNCULACEAE. *Buttercup or Crowfoot Family*

THIMBLE WEED (*Anemone riparia*).

1. Upper part of plant, x 1. 2. Cluster of achenes breaking apart, x 1.

Flowers greenish-white, white, or rarely reddish; stems 1–3 ft. tall, 1 or more from the crown. Dry, open woods, thickets, and prairies. Widely distributed in the state, but still unrecorded in large sections of the northeastern and southwestern quarters. Two other species of thimble weed found in the state, *A. cylindrica* and *A. virginiana*, are very similar to this one.

RANUNCULACEAE. Buttercup or Crowfoot Family

RUE ANEMONE (*Anemonella thalictroides*).

1–2. Habit of plant, x 1.

Flowers pink to purplish or white; stems 3–8 in. tall; roots thickened. Dry, open woods. In southeastern Minnesota, east of a line joining Chisago, Scott, Rice, and Fillmore counties.

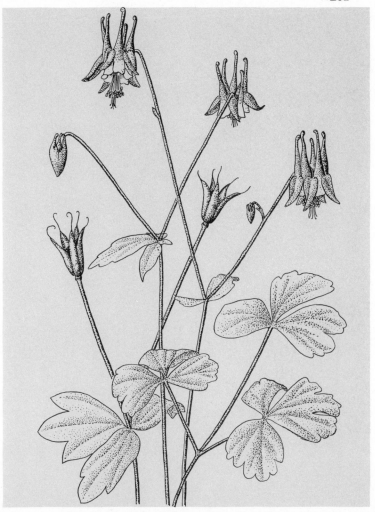

RANUNCULACEAE. *Buttercup or Crowfoot Family*

WILD COLUMBINE (*Aquilegia canadensis*).

Upper part of plant, x ¾.

Sepals and petal spurs usually reddish; petals yellow or yellowish; stems mostly 1–3 ft. tall; short-lived perennial. Very cosmopolitan, in moist to dry habitats. Found throughout the state; our only native columbine.

RANUNCULACEAE. Buttercup or Crowfoot Family

MARSH MARIGOLD; COWSLIP (*Caltha palustris*).

Upper part of plant, x ¾.

Flowers bright yellow; stems 0.5–1.5 ft. tall, succulent when young. Sunny marshes, stream margins, and wet, open woods. Throughout the state, but rare in or absent from most of the prairie counties of the south and west.

RANUNCULACEAE. Buttercup or Crowfoot Family

GOLDTHREAD (*Coptis groenlandica*).

Habit of plant, x 1.

Flowers white; spreading by slender, yellow root-stocks. Moist woods and bogs. In our state, north and east of a line joining Hennepin, Becker, Clearwater, and Lake of the Woods counties; also reported from Blue Earth County.

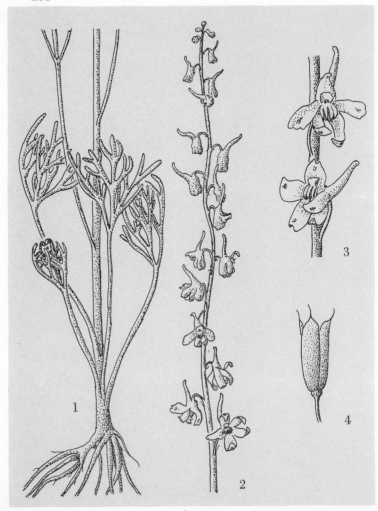

RANUNCULACEAE. *Buttercup or Crowfoot Family*

PRAIRIE LARKSPUR (*Delphinium virescens*).

1–2. Habit of plant, x ½. 3. Flowers, x 1. 4. Fruit, x 1.

Flowers purplish or greenish-white; stems 1–4 or more ft. tall. Dry, open hillsides, prairies, and oak savannah. In the southwestern three-fifths of the state, south and west of a line joining Chisago, Crow Wing, Becker, and Polk counties.

RANUNCULACEAE. *Buttercup or Crowfoot Family*

SHARP-LOBED LIVERLEAF (*Hepatica acutiloba*).

1. Habit in early spring, x 1. 2. Mature leaf, x 1.

Flowers pinkish to bluish, white or purplish. Moist to dry upland woods. Southeastern Minnesota, south and east of a line connecting Washington, Morrison, and Nicollet counties.

ROUND-LOBED LIVERLEAF (*Hepatica americana*).

3. Mature leaf, x 1.

Recognized chiefly by the leaves. Found in similar habitats in southeastern, central, and northeastern Minnesota east of a line connecting Fillmore, northeastern Otter Tail, southern Clearwater, and Koochiching counties.

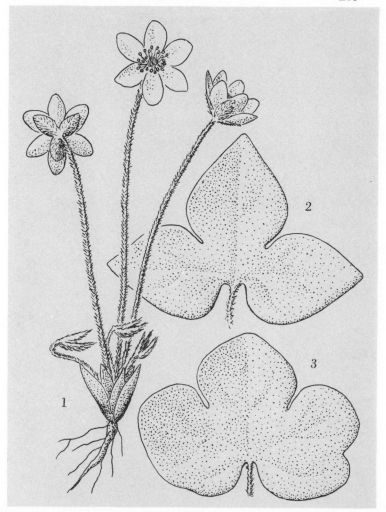

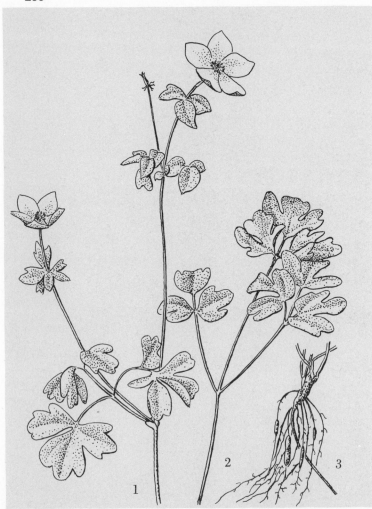

1
2
3

RANUNCULACEAE. *Buttercup or Crowfoot Family*

FALSE RUE ANEMONE (*Isopyrum biternatum*).

1. Upper part of plant, x 1. 2. Leaf, x 1. 3. Root system, x 1.

Flowers white; stems 0.5–1.5 ft. tall, loosely grouped or 1 at a place. Rich, moist woods. Southeastern Minnesota, south and east of a line joining Hennepin, Blue Earth, and Mower counties.

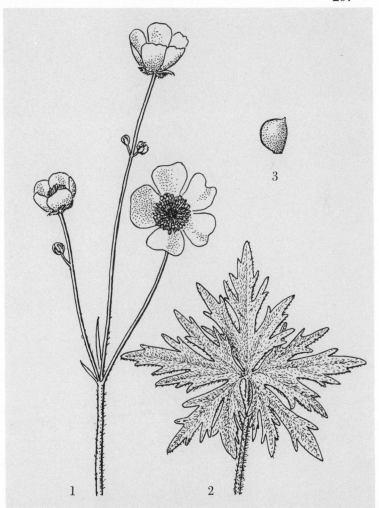

RANUNCULACEAE. *Buttercup or Crowfoot Family*

TALL OR MEADOW BUTTERCUP (*Ranunculus acris*).

1. Inflorescence, x 1. 2. Basal leaf, x ½.
3. Achene, x 4.

Flowers yellow; stems mostly 1.0–2.5 ft. tall, usually with long, spreading hairs. Fields, meadows, and roadsides; a native of Europe, but now fully naturalized. In the eastern half of the state west to Kandiyohi and Lake of the Woods counties; absent from the southern 2 tiers of counties except Houston County. Numerous native but less conspicuous species of buttercup are found in the state.

RANUNCULACEAE. *Buttercup or Crowfoot Family*

PRAIRIE BUTTERCUP; CROWFOOT (*Ranunculus rhomboideus*).

Upper part of plant, x 1.

Flowers yellow; stems mostly 3–8 in. tall, the stems and leaves loosely hairy throughout. Open woods, hills, and prairies. Widespread south and west of a line joining Washington, Crow Wing, and Kittson counties; also reported from Roseau and Lake of the Woods counties.

RANUNCULACEAE. *Buttercup or Crowfoot Family*

SWAMP BUTTERCUP (*Ranunculus septentrionalis*).

1–2. Habit, x ½. 3. Achene, x 6.

Petals bright yellow; young stems more or less erect at first, sprawling as they grow longer with age. Low, wet woods and meadows. In the eastern half of the state, west to Faribault, Waseca, and Roseau counties; isolated records from Pipestone and Chippewa counties.

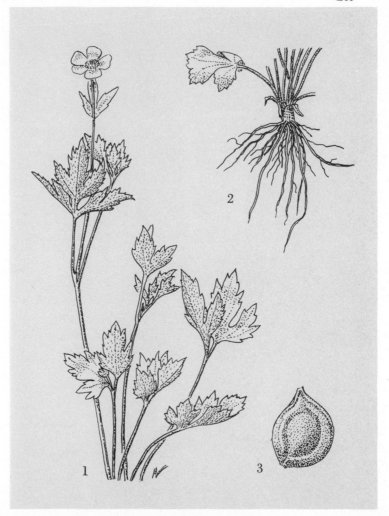

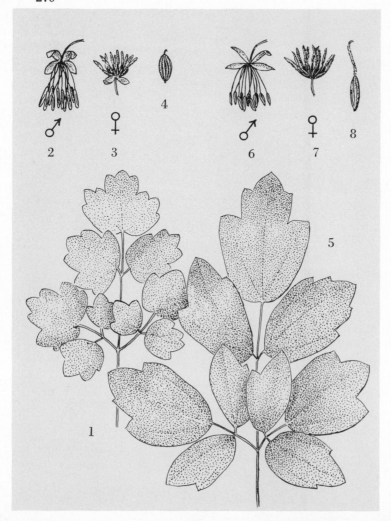

2 ♂   3 ♀   4   6 ♂   7 ♀   8   5   1

RANUNCULACEAE. Buttercup or Crowfoot Family

EARLY MEADOW RUE (*Thalictrum dioicum*).

1. Leaf, x 1. 2. Staminate flower, x 2. 3. Pistillate flower, x 2. 4. Single mature achene, x 2.

Flowers greenish-yellow or purplish; stems 1–2 ft. tall, 1 or more from the crown; plants usually of 2 kinds, those bearing only staminate and those bearing only pistillate flowers. Moist woods. Throughout the wooded parts of the state.

TALL MEADOW RUE (*Thalictrum dasycarpum*).

5. Leaf, x 1. 6. Staminate flower, x 2. 7. Pistillate flower, x 2. 8. A single mature achene, x 2.

Flowers greenish or purplish; stems to about 5 ft. tall, often purplish, coarse, usually only 1 from the crown; plants of 2 kinds, as above. Wet meadows, swamps, and stream banks. Throughout the state.

RANUNCULACEAE. Buttercup or Crowfoot Family

EARLY MEADOW RUE (*Thalictrum dioicum*).

Upper part of staminate plant, x 1.

For more details, see the preceding illustration.

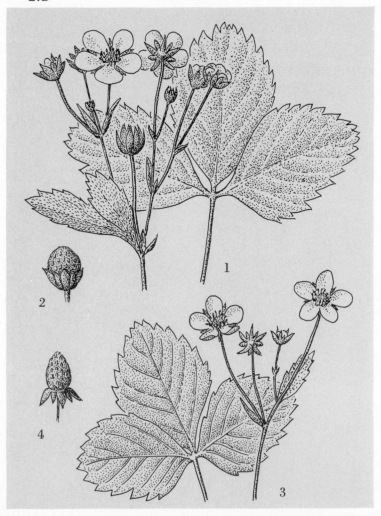

ROSACEAE. *Rose Family*

VIRGINIA STRAWBERRY (*Fragaria virginiana*).

1. Inflorescence and leaf, x 1. 2. Fruit, x 1.

Petals white; achenes or "seeds" at the bottom of little pits in the surface of the fruit; spreading by runners or stolons. Open woods and thickets. Common throughout the state.

WOODLAND STRAWBERRY (*Fragaria vesca*).

3. Inflorescence and leaf, x 1. 4. Fruit, x 1.

Much like the preceding, but the achenes on the surface of the fruit. Open woods and thickets. Generally distributed in the state except in the northwestern corner.

ROSACEAE. *Rose Family*

WATER OR PURPLE AVENS (*Geum rivale*).

1. Habit, x ¼. 2. Cluster of achenes, x 1. 3. Inflorescence, x 1. 4. Basal leaf, x ½.

Petals yellowish or tinged with purple; sepals purple or yellowish or greenish. Bogs and wet meadows. In the northeastern two-fifths of the state, north and east of a line connecting Chisago, northern Wright, eastern Otter Tail, Clearwater, and Lake of the Woods counties.

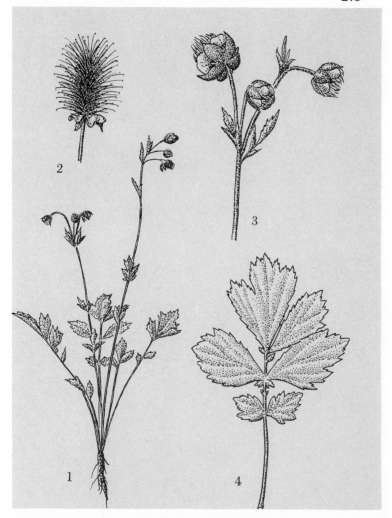

274

ROSACEAE. *Rose Family*

PURPLE AVENS (*Geum triflorum*).

Habit, x ⅓. For details, see the next illustration.

Sepals purple; petals pale yellow to purplish; stems and leaves loosely hairy; plants spreading from the crown and forming compact colonies. Moist to dry prairies. In the southern and western three-fifths of the state, south and west of a line joining Washington, Isanti, southern Clearwater, and Roseau counties; also reported from Lake County.

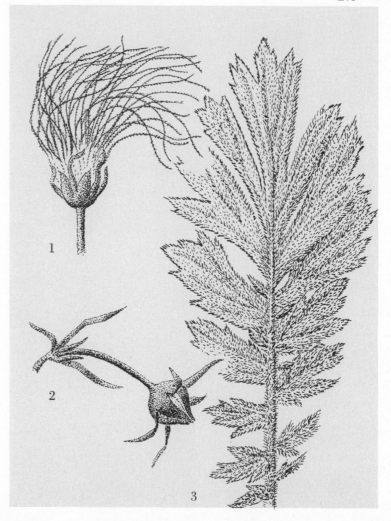

ROSACEAE. *Rose Family*

PURPLE AVENS (*Geum triflorum*).

1. Flower, with ripe achenes, showing brushlike mass of styles, x 1. 2. Bud just before opening, x 1. 3. Basal leaf, x 1.

For further details, see the preceding illustration.

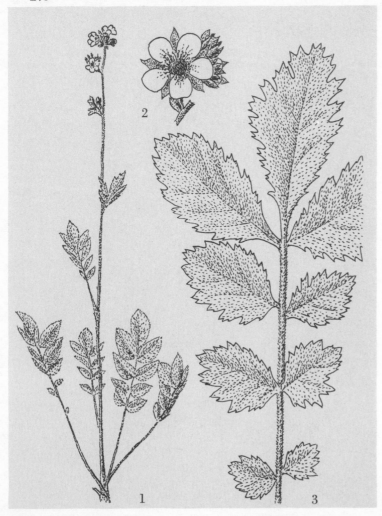

ROSACEAE. Rose Family

TALL CINQUEFOIL (*Potentilla arguta*).

1. Habit, x ¼. 2. Cluster of flowers, x 1. 3. Basal leaf, x 1.

Petals white to pale yellow; stems mostly 1.0–2.5 ft. tall; stems and leaves sticky and loosely hairy. Open woods and prairies, often in sandy soil. Seen throughout the state.

ROSACEAE. Rose Family

MARSH CINQUEFOIL (*Potentilla palustris*).

1. Upper part of stem, x 1. 2. Section of stem with leaf base and adventitious roots, x 1. 3. Basal leaf, x ½.

Petals red-purple; stems prostrate, but turning up at the tips, mostly 0.5–1.5 ft. long, nearly smooth. Bogs, sloughs, sedge mats, and other very wet places. Generally distributed in the northeastern two-fifths of the state, then southward to Waseca and Redwood counties and west to Otter Tail, Becker, and northeastern Roseau counties.

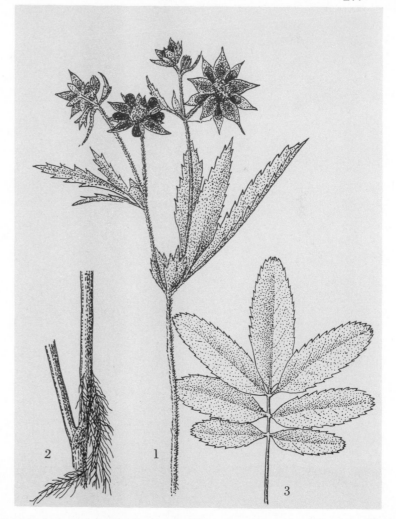

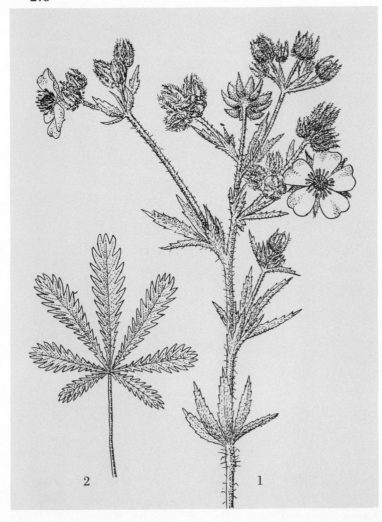

2 1

ROSACEAE. Rose Family

CINQUEFOIL (*Potentilla recta*).

1. Upper half of stem, x 1. 2. Basal leaf, x ½.

Petals pale yellow; stems mostly 1–2 ft. tall, 1 or more from the crown. Old fields and dry pastures; introduced from Europe and spreading rapidly. Found at widely scattered localities in the southeastern, central, and northern parts of the state. The common name cinquefoil is used indiscriminately for many different species of *Potentilla*.

ROSACEAE. *Rose Family*

OLD-FIELD CINQUEFOIL (*Potentilla simplex*).

1. Outer end of stem, x 1. 2. Flower from the back, x 2.

Petals yellow; stems erect while young, but, as they grow older, they become arched or prostrate and root at the tips, ultimately 3 ft. or more in length, loosely hairy. Dry fields and open woods. Present in southern, central, and northeastern Minnesota, east of a line joining Jackson, Renville, western Morrison, and northern St. Louis counties.

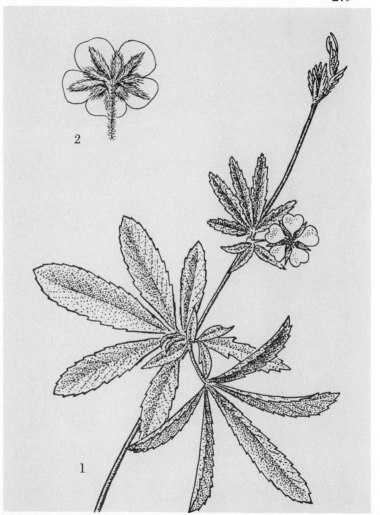

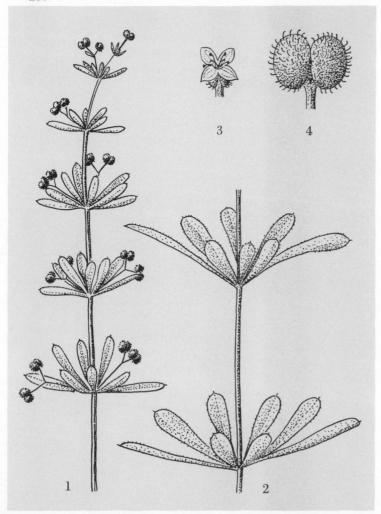

3

4

1

2

RUBIACEAE. *Madder Family*

CLEAVERS (*Galium aparine*).

1. Outer portion of stem with fruits, x 1. 2. Middle section of stem, x 1. 3. Flower, x 5. 4. Fruit, x 5.

Flowers white; stems weak, reclining or clambering over other plants, very rough because of the backward-pointing, small bristles; plants annual. Damp soil, woods, and thickets, in full or partial shade. In southern and central Minnesota, south of a line joining Itasca and Norman counties; commonest in the southern third of the state.

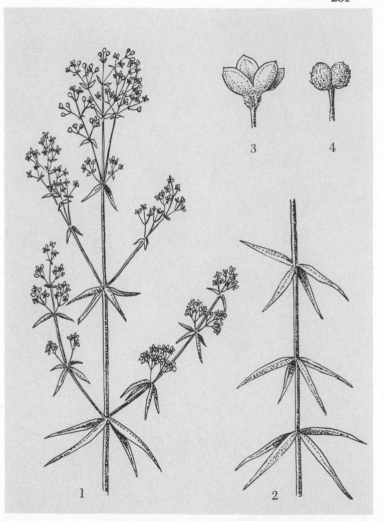

RUBIACEAE. *Madder Family*

NORTHERN BEDSTRAW (*Galium boreale*).

1. Inflorescence, x ½. 2. Middle section of stem, x ½. 3. Flower, x 5. 4. Fruit, x 5.

Flowers white or pale yellowish; stems mostly 1–2 ft. tall, erect, usually several from the crown. Moist, open woods and meadows. Distributed throughout the state.

2

3

1

RUBIACEAE. Madder Family

HOUSTONIA (*Houstonia longifolia*).

1. Habit, x 1. 2. Flower, x 2. 3. Capsule, x 2.

Flowers pale blue, purplish, or whitish; stems 1 or more from the perennial base. Moist to dry places, loose, well-drained soils, in full or nearly full sun. Widely distributed in the state, except in the west-central and southern border counties.

SANTALACEAE. *Sandalwood Family*

BASTARD TOADFLAX (*Comandra umbellata*).

1–2. Habit, x 1. 3. Inflorescence in fruit, x 1.

Flowers whitish; stems mostly 0.5–1.0 ft. tall, a little branched at the top, arising singly from a buried, underground rootstock and forming small to large colonies; herbage bluish. Prairies and openings in woods. Throughout the state.

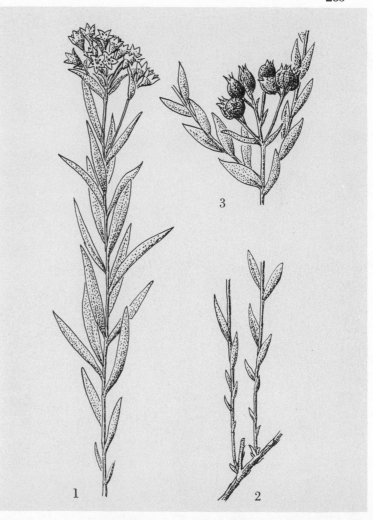

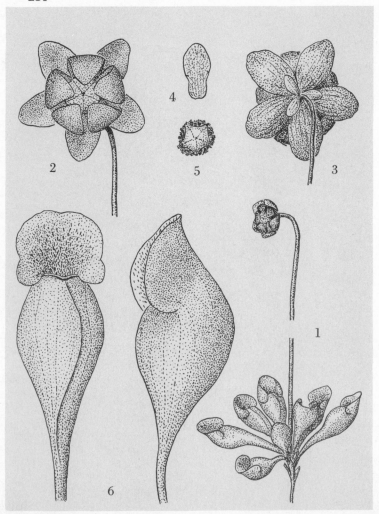

SARRACENIACEAE. Pitcher Plant Family

PITCHER PLANT (*Sarracenia purpurea*).

1. Habit, x ⅛. 2. Face view of flower, x ½. 3. Flower from back, x ½. 4. Petal, x ½. 5. Stigma and stamens, x ½. 6. Leaf seen from above and from the side, x ½.

Flowers purple or partly greenish- or yellowish-purple. Sphagnum bogs and floating sedge mats. Found mainly in the northeastern quarter of the state; all records from north and east of a line joining Scott, southeastern Clearwater, and the Lake of the Woods counties.

SAXIFRAGACEAE. *Saxifrage Family*

HEUCHERA; ALUM ROOT (*Heuchera richardsonii*).

1. Inflorescence, x 1. 2. Flower, x 4. 3. Fruit, x 4.
4. Basal leaf, x 1.

Flowers greenish or purplish; flowering stems
mostly 1–2 ft. tall, usually several from a thick,
branched, perennial crown; leaves basal. Moist prairies, open woods, cliffs, and banks. Found throughout
the state. This is our only alum root native to Minnesota. The common name is widely used for other
species of *Heuchera*, both wild and cultivated.

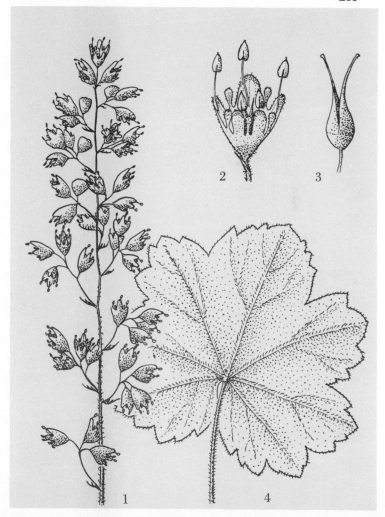

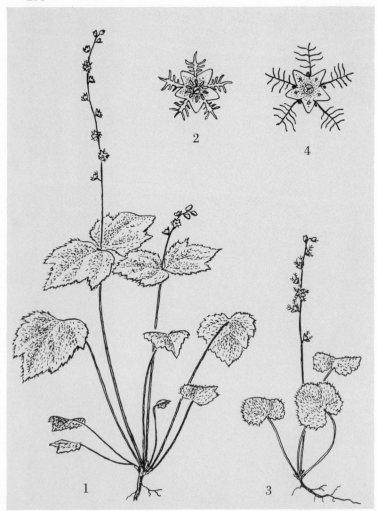

SAXIFRAGACEAE. Saxifrage Family

BISHOP'S CAP; MITREWORT (*Mitella diphylla*).

1. Habit, x ½. 2. Face view of flower, x 3.

Flowers white; flowering stems mostly 0.5–1.5 ft. tall; stems and leaves loosely and sparsely hairy. Rich, shady woods, in moist, organic soil. Found in central and eastern Minnesota in an area bounded by a line joining Mower, Blue Earth, eastern Mahnomen, southern Itasca, and southern St. Louis counties.

BISHOP'S CAP; MITREWORT (*Mitella nuda*).

3. Habit, x ½. 4. Face view of flower, x 3.

Flowers yellowish-green; stem leaves lacking; plants spreading by slender stolons. Moist to wet woods and bogs. Present north and east of a line joining Rice, Douglas, Mahnomen, and Roseau counties.

SAXIFRAGACEAE. *Saxifrage Family*

GRASS OF PARNASSUS (*Parnassia glauca*).

1. Habit, x ½. 2. Flower, x ½. 3. Staminodium, x 1.
4. Petal, x 1.

Petals white with greenish or yellowish veins; leaves bluish-green, thick and fleshy, rounded or shallowly notched at the base. Wet meadows and shores, calcareous soils. Found in a narrow strip joining Houston and Clay counties and then to Kittson and Beltrami counties.

GRASS OF PARNASSUS (*Parnassia palustris*).

5. Habit, x ½. 6. Flower, x ½. 7. Staminodium, x 1.

Petals as above; leaves thin, usually heart-shaped at the base. Habitat as above. In central and northern Minnesota, north of a line connecting Anoka, Kandiyohi, and Clay counties.

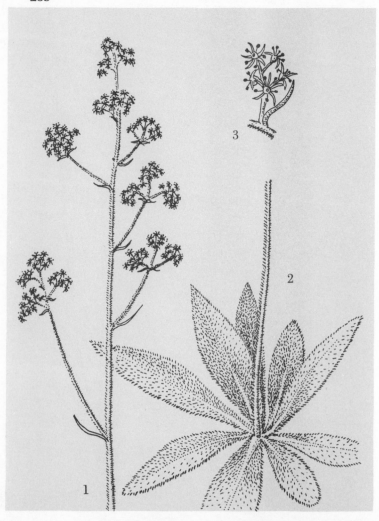

SAXIFRAGACEAE. *Saxifrage Family*

SWAMP SAXIFRAGE (*Saxifraga pensylvanica*).
1–2. Habit, x ¼. 3. Cluster of flowers, x 1.

Petals greenish-yellow or whitish; flowering stems mostly 1.0–2.5 ft. tall; leaves all basal. Wet meadows and swamps. Eastern and central Minnesota, east of a line joining Houston, Olmsted, Scott, Otter Tail, southern Clearwater, southern Beltrami, and the southern half of St. Louis counties; not recorded from Lake or Cook counties.

SCROPHULARIACEAE. *Figwort Family*

PAINTED CUP; INDIAN PAINT BRUSH (*Castilleja coccinea*).

1. Habit, x ½. 2. Inflorescence, x 1.

Floral bracts bright scarlet toward the tip or of various shades to yellow; corolla pale greenish-yellow; stems 1 to several from the crown, loosely hairy; plants annual or biennial. Meadows, moist prairies, and open woodlands. Distributed in southeastern, central, and northern Minnesota north and east of a line joining Houston, Waseca, Meeker, and Clay counties. Another Indian paint brush, the downy painted cup occurs in the dry prairies of the state south and west of a line joining Washington, Pope, Mahnomen, and Kittson counties. It is a perennial of shorter stature, with ashy-gray foliage, green floral bracts, and yellowish-white corollas.

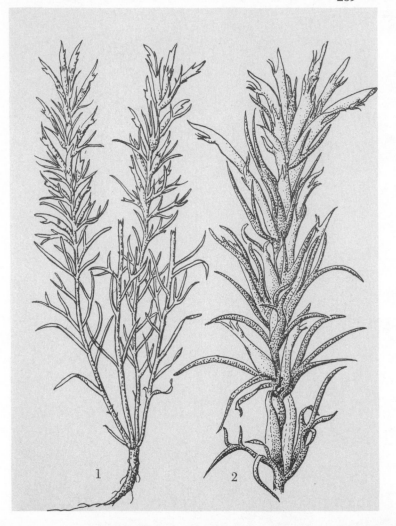

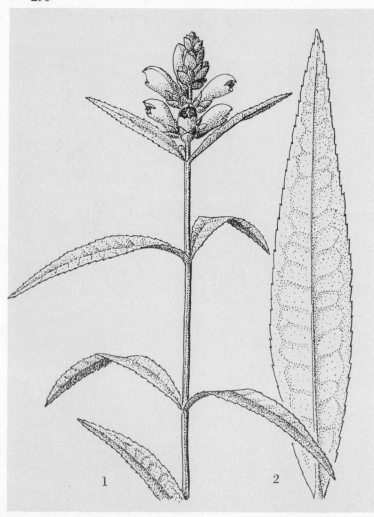

1   2

SCROPHULARIACEAE. *Figwort Family*

TURTLEHEAD (*Chelone glabra*).

1. Upper part of stem, x ½. 2. Leaf, x 1.

Corolla white or greenish-yellow, or tinged with pink; stems coarse, mostly 1–3 ft. tall, 1 or more from the crown. Wet, low meadows and woods. Found mostly in the eastern third of the state, but a few records from as far west as Blue Earth, southern Clearwater, and Roseau counties.

SCROPHULARIACEAE. *Figwort Family*

GERARDIA (*Gerardia aspera*).

1. Upper part of stem at flowering time, x 1. 2. Upper part of stem in fruit, x 1.

Corolla purple; stems, mostly 1–2 ft. tall, rough. Wet prairies. Present in southern and western Minnesota south and west of a line joining Goodhue, Hennepin, Otter Tail, and Polk counties. This is the largest of several species of *Gerardia* found in the state. They are distinguished by small, technical differences.

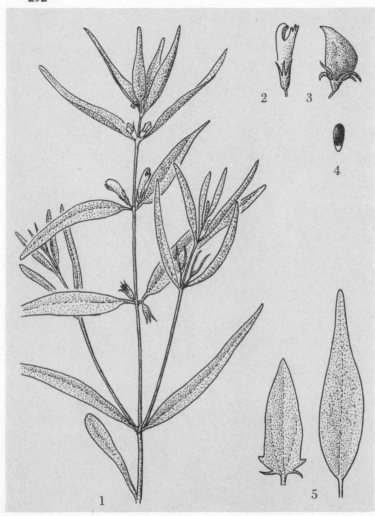

2 3

4

1 5

SCROPHULARIACEAE. *Figwort Family*

COW WHEAT (*Melampyrum lineare*).

1. Upper part of plant, x 1. 2. Flower, x 2. 3. Capsule, x 2. 4. Seed, x 2. 5. Middle stem leaves, x 1.

Corolla greenish- or yellowish-white; stems mostly 0.5–1.0 ft. high, widely branched. Often in dry coniferous forests or in duff at the edges of bogs. Common in northeastern Minnesota within an area bounded by a line joining Carlton, western Morrison, southern Clearwater, and eastern Roseau counties.

SCROPHULARIACEAE. *Figwort Family*

MONKEY FLOWER (*Mimulus ringens*).

Upper half of stem, x 1.

Corolla blue or violet; plants mostly 1.0–2.5 ft. tall, smooth; stem square in cross-section. Stream banks, lakeshores, swamps, and very wet meadows. Found throughout the state. Another smaller monkey flower, *M. glabratus*, with proportionately broader leaves and yellow corolla, sometimes with reddish flecks, is found mainly in counties adjacent to the Mississippi River and its tributaries, from Clearwater to Houston counties (also reported from Rock County). It grows in cold springs and seepages or in quiet backwaters of cold streams.

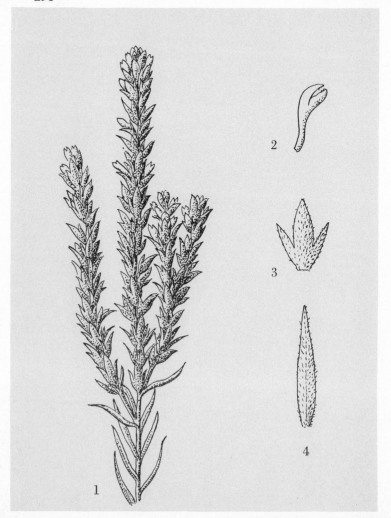

SCROPHULARIACEAE. *Figwort Family*

ORTHOCARPUS (*Orthocarpus luteus*).

1. Upper part of stem, x 1. 2. Corolla, x 2. 3. Floral bract, x 2. 4. Stem leaf, x 2.

Corolla yellow; stems 0.5–1.5 ft. tall; plants annual. Dry prairies. Northwestern Minnesota, northwest of a line joining Polk and Lake of the Woods counties; also recorded from southern St. Louis and Pipestone counties.

SCROPHULARIACEAE. *Figwort Family*

COMMON LOUSEWORT; WOOD BETONY (*Pedicularis canadensis*).

1. Upper part of stem, x 1. 2. Lower stem leaf, x 1.
3. Inflorescence in fruit, x 1.

Corolla usually yellow, sometimes reddish or purplish; stems 0.5–1.5 ft. tall, loosely hairy. Upland woods, meadows, and prairies. Very common south and west of a line joining Chisago, southern Itasca, and Kittson counties. Another similar, but larger, lousewort, *P. lanceolata*, grows in very wet meadows south and west of a line joining southern Pine and Roseau counties.

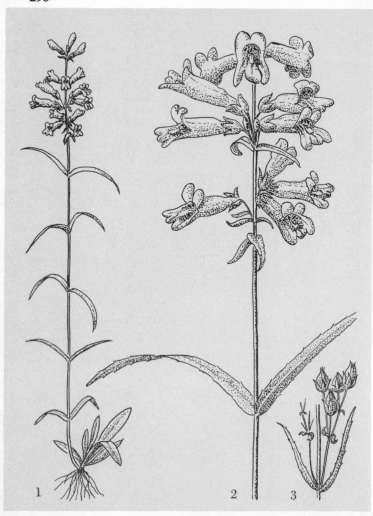

1 2 3

SCROPHULARIACEAE. *Figwort Family*

BEARD-TONGUE (*Penstemon gracilis*).

1. Habit, x ⅓. 2. Upper part of stem, x 1.
3. Capsules, x 1.

Corolla lavender; stems mostly 0.5–1.5 ft. tall. Open
woods and prairies. Found over large areas of the
state, but rare in the northeastern quarter and along
the Iowa border. Another species of beard-tongue,
P. albidus, is found on the dry prairies of western
Minnesota. Its corolla is white, rarely tinged with
violet, and some of the hairs on the inside of the
corolla have bulbous tips. The common name given
is used, not only for the 3 species native to Minnesota but also for all of the very numerous species
of the genus *Penstemon*.

SCROPHULARIACEAE. *Figwort Family*

LARGE-FLOWERED BEARD-TONGUE (*Penstemon grandiflorus*).

1. Habit, x ¼. 2. Inflorescence, x ¾. 3. Capsule, x ¾.

Corolla pale purple; stems 1.0–2.5 ft. or more tall; stems and leaves waxy-blue, entirely smooth; leaves thick and leathery. Prairies, mostly in sandy soil. Eastern, central, and western Minnesota from southern St. Louis County to Polk County in the north and from northern Goodhue County west to Rock County in the south. One of our most beautiful wild flowers but, unfortunately, very difficult to maintain in gardens.

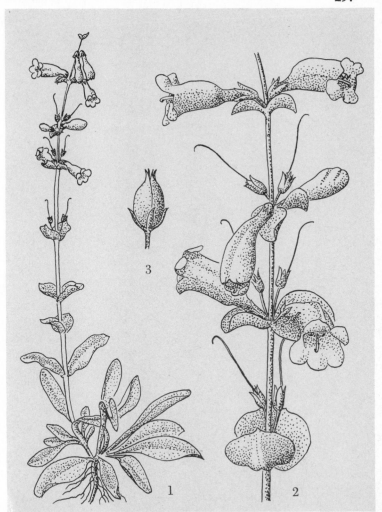

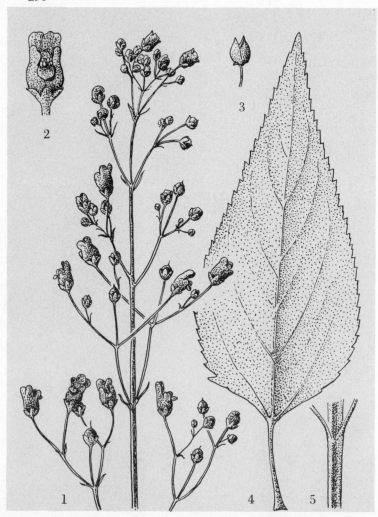

SCROPHULARIACEAE. *Figwort Family*

FIGWORT (*Scrophularia lanceolata*).

1. Inflorescence, x 1. 2. Face view of flower, x 2. 3. Capsule, x 1. 4. Stem leaf, x 1. 5. Upper node of stem, x 1.

Corolla greenish- or reddish-brown, shiny; stems often 5 ft. or more tall, 4-sided in cross-section, with flattened sides, very coarse, 1 to several from the crown; leaves paired at each node of the stem. Thickets, open woods, and old fields. To be expected in all counties of the state, but commonest in the south and east.

SCROPHULARIACEAE. *Figwort Family*

COMMON MULLEIN (*Verbascum thapsus*).

1. Upper part of stem in late flower, x ⅛. 2. Tip of inflorescence with flowers and capsules, x 1. 3. Face view of flower, x 1. 4. Section of stem, x 1.

Corolla yellow; stems to 5–6 ft. tall; stems and leaves covered with dense white wool throughout; plants biennial. Old fields, pastures, and roadsides; native of Europe and generally considered to be a weed although the plants are rather attractive when in flower. Widely distributed in the state except, perhaps, in the prairie counties to the west; commonest in the southeastern quarter.

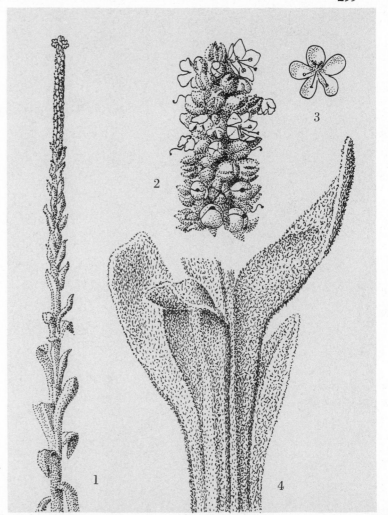

1

2

3   4

SCROPHULARIACEAE. *Figwort Family*

AMERICAN BROOKLIME; SPEEDWELL (*Veronica americana*).

1. Upper part of stem, x 1. 2. Middle section of stem, with adventitious roots, x 1. 3. Face view of flower, x 2. 4. Capsule, x 2.

Corolla blue-violet to lilac; stems creeping, turned upward at the tip, succulent, entirely smooth; leaves with short stalks. Wet, cool habitats in swamps and along waterways. In Minnesota, east of a line joining Houston, Pope, and Lake of the Woods counties. Another similar species, *V. comosa*, with stalkless leaves is found in slow-moving streams and backwaters at widely separated localities in the state.

SCROPHULARIACEAE. *Figwort Family*

CULVER'S ROOT (*Veronicastrum virginicum*).

1. Upper part of stem, x ¼. 2. Branch of the inflorescence, x ¾. 3. Flower, x 2. 4. Leaf, x ¾.

Corolla white or purplish; stems to 5 ft. or more tall. Moist to dry woods, thickets, and prairies. To be expected in almost all counties of the state, but evidently rare in the northeastern quarter.

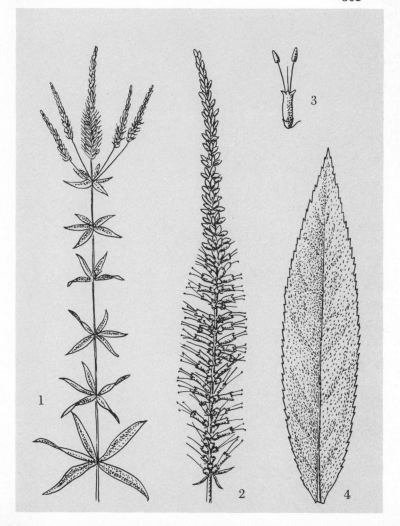

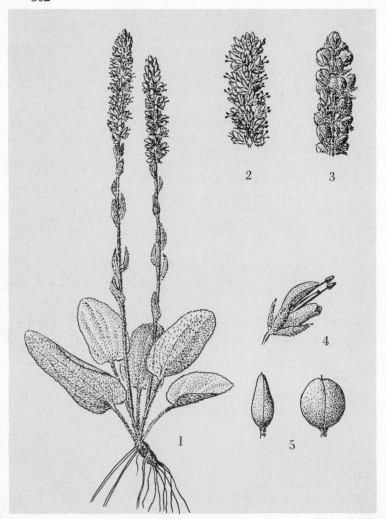

SCROPHULARIACEAE. *Figwort Family*

SYNTHYRIS (*Wulfenia bullii*; *Besseya bullii*).
1. Habit, x ½. 2. Tip of inflorescence in flower, x 1.
3. Tip of inflorescence in fruit, x 1. 4. Side view of
flower, x 3. 5. Two views of the capsule, x 3.

Corolla greenish- or yellowish-white. Sandy, dry
prairies. In Minnesota, confined to a small triangle
formed by a line joining northern Washington,
northern Scott, and northern Goodhue counties.

SOLANACEAE. *Potato Family*

GROUND CHERRY (*Physalis virginiana*).

1. Upper part of stem, x 1. 2. Bladderlike calyx with berry inside, x 1.

Corolla dull yellow with brown center; stems 0.5–1.0 ft. or more high, arising singly from a deep subterranean rootstock; forming small colonies; berry greenish-yellow. Open, dry woods and prairies. In southern and western Minnesota south and west of a line joining northern Washington, Crow Wing, southern Beltrami, and Kittson counties; also recorded from southern St. Louis County. The clammy ground cherry, *P. heterophylla*, is also common south of a line joining southern St. Louis and Clay counties. It has broader leaves with wavier margins and longer hairs on the stem. The hairs secrete a sticky substance.

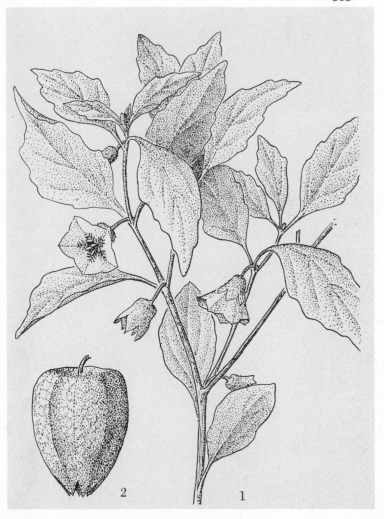

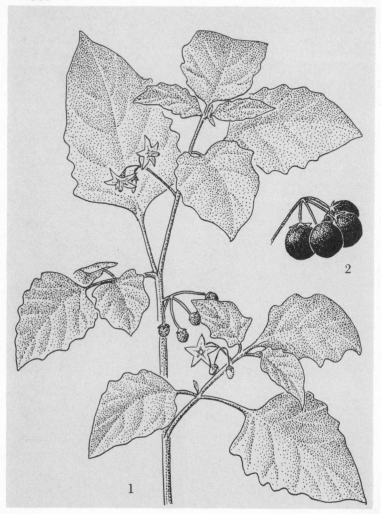

1

2

SOLANACEAE. *Potato Family*

BLACK NIGHTSHADE (*Solanum nigrum*).

1. Upper part of stem, x 1. 2. Berries, x 1.

Flowers white or tinged with purple; stems widely branched, mostly 1.0–1.5 ft. tall; berries bluish-black when ripe; annual; poisonous, at least sometimes. Roadsides and waste places. Throughout the state.

UMBELLIFERAE. *Carrot or Parsley Family*

WATER HEMLOCK (*Cicuta maculata*).

1. Upper part of stem, x ⅓. 2. Face view of flower, x 3. 3. Fruit, x 3. 4. Lower stem leaf, x ⅓.

Flower clusters white; stems to 6 ft. or more high, often mottled with purple; roots thick and fleshy; very poisonous. Very wet soil, meadows, margins of water courses and road ditches. Throughout the state.

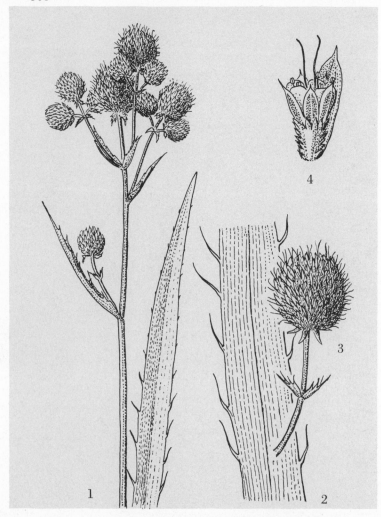

UMBELLIFERAE. *Carrot or Parsley Family*

BUTTON SNAKEROOT; RATTLESNAKE MASTER
(*Eryngium yuccifolium*).

1. Top of stem and tip of leaf, x ½. 2. Middle section from leaf, x 1. 3. Flowering head, x 1. 4. A single flower from the head, x 4.

Flowers white, in compact heads; stems 1.5–5.0 ft. or more tall. Moist or dry soil, open woods, and prairies. Southeastern Minnesota, south and east of a line joining northern Goodhue, Brown, and Martin counties.

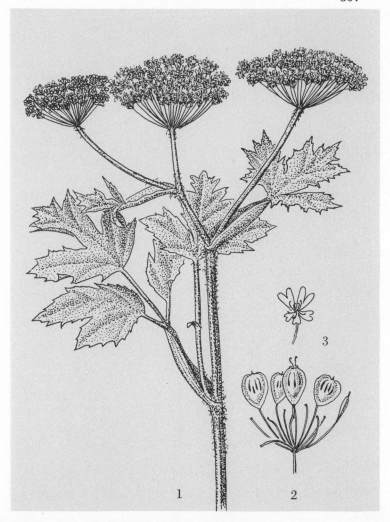

UMBELLIFERAE. *Carrot or Parsley Family*

COW PARSNIP (*Heracleum maximum*).

1. Upper part of stem, x ¼. 2. Umbellet in fruit, x 1.
3. Flower, x 1.

Flower clusters white or purplish; stems 3–6 ft. or
more tall, covered with long hair. Low ground, rich
soil, in open sun. Throughout the state.

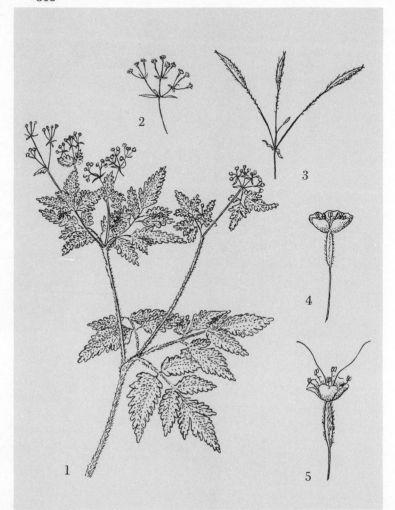

UMBELLIFERAE. *Carrot or Parsley Family*

SWEET CICELY (*Osmorhiza claytoni*).

1. Upper part of stem, x ¼. 2. Umbel, in flower, x 1.
3. Umbellet, in fruit, x 1. 4. Flower, x 6.

Flower clusters white, the styles scarcely visible at
first; stems mostly 1–3 ft. tall; root only slightly
fleshy, only a little fragrant. Rich woods. In forested
areas throughout the state, but commonest in the
southeastern quarter.

ANISE ROOT; SWEET CICELY (*Osmorhiza longistylis*).

5. Flower, x 6.

Similar to *O. claytoni*, but the long, slender styles are
clearly visible at flowering time; roots more fleshy
and having a strong anise scent. Habitat and
distribution the same.

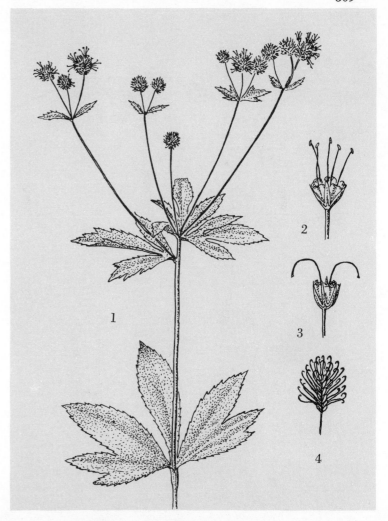

UMBELLIFERAE. *Carrot or Parsley Family*

BLACK SNAKEROOT; SANICLE (*Sanicula marilandica*).

1. Upper part of stem, x ½. 2. Staminate flower, x 4. 3. Perfect flower, x 4. 4. Fruit, x 4.

Flowers greenish-white, in compact clusters; stems 1–3 ft. tall; basal leaves with long stalks palmately divided mostly into 5 divisions. Woodlands and thickets. Throughout the state. We have 3 more kinds of *Sanicula* within our borders, all of which bear the same common names.

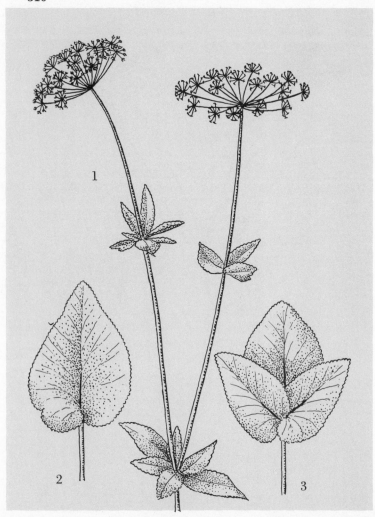

1

2

3

UMBELLIFERAE. *Carrot or Parsley Family*

HEART-LEAVED ALEXANDERS (*Zizia aptera*).

1. Upper part of stem, x ½. 2. Basal leaf, x ½.
3. Lower stem leaf, x ½.

Flowers yellow; stems 1–2 ft. tall, smooth; leaves leathery. Moist meadows, prairies, and open woods. Throughout the state.

UMBELLIFERAE. *Carrot or Parsley Family*

GOLDEN ALEXANDERS (*Zizia aurea*).

1. Upper part of stem, x ½. 2. Basal leaf, x ½.

Flowers yellow; stems mostly 1–2 ft. tall, smooth; leaves of ordinary texture. Moist to wet meadows and thickets. Throughout the state.

312

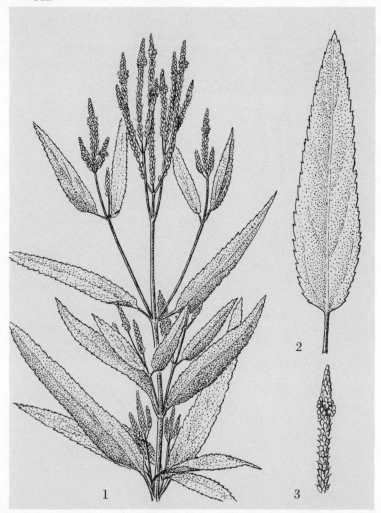

1

2

3

VERBENACEAE. *Vervain Family*

BLUE VERVAIN (*Verbena hastata*).

1. Upper part of stem, x ½. 2. Stem leaf, x 1. 3. Tip of inflorescence branch, x 1.

Corolla blue or sometimes violet or pink; spikes flowering progressively from the base to the top; stems 1.5–4.5 ft. tall. Pastures, wet meadows, and swamps. Found throughout the state.

VERBENACEAE. *Vervain Family*

HOARY VERVAIN (*Verbena stricta*).

1. Upper half of stem, x ¼. 2. Stem leaf, x 1. 3. Upper part of inflorescence branch, x 1. 4. Calyx with ovary within, the latter breaking apart, x 2. 5. Flower, x 2.

Corolla purple, deep blue, or rarely pink; spikes flower progressively from base to top; stems stout, 1–3 ft. tall, often clumped; stems and leaves with a dense cover of gray hair. Moist to dry prairies and barren fields. Found in the southern and southwestern parts of the state, south and west of a line joining Washington and Clay counties; also reported from near Duluth.

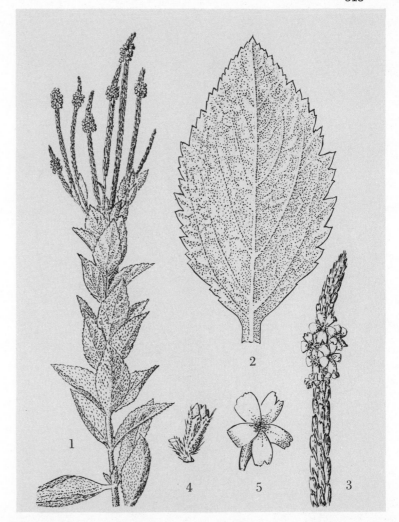

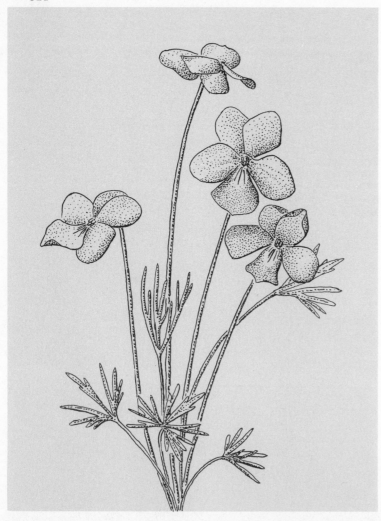

VIOLACEAE. Violet Family

BIRD'S-FOOT OR PANSY VIOLET (*Viola pedata*).
Above-ground parts, x 1.

Petals ranging from blue to purple, the upper 2 sometimes much darker than the lower 3; stemless. Open, dry, usually sandy soil. Southeastern Minnesota, south and east of a line joining northern Washington, Anoka, western Dakota, and Mower counties. A similar species, the prairie or bearded bird's-foot violet, *V. pedatifida*, is found in the prairies of southern and western Minnesota, south and west of a line joining northern Washington, central Beltrami, and Kittson counties. This one has violet petals and the 3 lower ones are bearded inside at the base.

VIOLACEAE. *Violet Family*

TALL WHITE VIOLET (*Viola rugulosa*).

1. Habit, x 1. 2. Capsule after splitting open, x 1.

Petals white inside, with yellowish eyespot and purplish veins, purplish outside; stems 0.5–1.0 ft. or more tall; colonial. Rich, shady woods. Generally distributed in the state; absent in the northeastern quarter except near the North Shore in St. Louis and Lake counties.

The common yellow violet, *V. pubescens*, is found over most of the state, especially in the eastern and central sections. It is similar to *V. rugulosa*, but the petals are yellow with purplish veins. It grows in the same habitats.

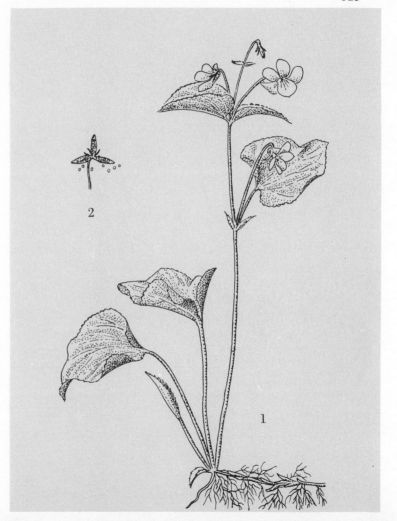

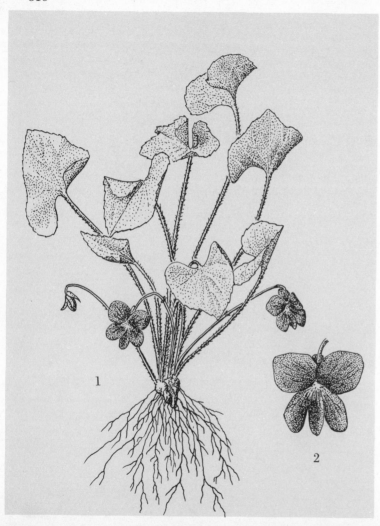

1

2

VIOLACEAE. *Violet Family*

COMMON OR WOOLLY BLUE VIOLET (*Viola sororia*).

1. Habit, x ½. 2. Face view of flower, x 1.

Petals violet to lavender or rarely white; stemless; under surfaces of young leaves and their stalks covered with dense spreading hair. Meadows and low woods. Found throughout the state. There are numerous violet species in the state (about 25), which are often difficult to distinguish without careful study.

Glossary

Glossary Figures

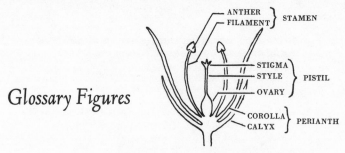

FIGURE 1. FLOWER IN SECTIONAL VIEW
(DIAGRAMMATIC)

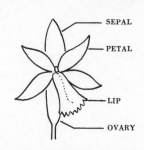

FIGURE 2. ORCHID FLOWER
(DIAGRAMMATIC)

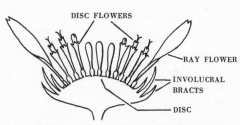

FIGURE 3. DIAGRAM OF TYPICAL COMPOSITE
HEAD, IN SECTIONAL VIEW

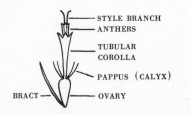

FIGURE 4. DISC FLOWER OF
COMPOSITE

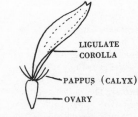

FIGURE 5. RAY FLOWER OF
COMPOSITE

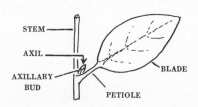

FIGURE 6. SIMPLE LEAF

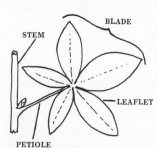

FIGURE 7. PALMATELY
COMPOUND LEAF

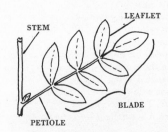

FIGURE 8. PINNATELY
COMPOUND LEAF

Glossary

Achene. A small, dry, 1-seeded fruit that does not split open at maturity.

Annual. Lasting for only 1 year; said of a plant that dies at the end of 1 growing season.

Adventitious root. One which arises directly from a stem.

Anther. The pollen-bearing part of a stamen. Figure 1.

Axil. The upper angle formed between an organ and the axis to which it is attached; e.g., between a leaf and a stem. Figure 6.

Beak. A stout, prolonged tip.

Beard. A tuft of stiffish hairs.

Berry. Strictly speaking, a pulpy or fleshy fruit formed from a single ovary and containing more than 1 seed; also used more casually to refer to various other fleshy fruit types such as the strawberry and raspberry.

Biennial. Lasting for 2 years; said of a plant that flowers and fruits in the second growing season from seed, after which it dies.

Bisexual. Having 1 or more functional pistils and stamens in the same flower.

Blade. The flattened part of an organ, especially a leaf. Figures 6–8.

Bract. A specialized leaf which differs in size, shape, texture, color, etc. from the foliage leaves of the same plant and which ordinarily subtends a flower or inflorescence. Figure 4.

Bristle. A long, stiff, hairlike structure.

Bulb. An underground structure consisting of closely overlapping, fleshy scales attached to a short axis.

Calyx. The outer series of floral organs when the perianth is differentiated into an outer and inner series. Figure 1.

Capsule. A dry, dehiscent fruit composed of 2 or more united carpels and usually containing 2 or more seeds.

Carpel. One of the unit structures which contains the ovules or seeds; they may occur singly or several in a flower and, when more than 1 to a flower, may be separate or united to form a compound ovary.

Clasping. Said of an organ such as a stalkless leaf whose line of attachment partially encircles the stem.

Cleistogamous. Refers to a specialized type of flower which does not open and consequently is self-pollinated; normally its perianth is not fully formed.

Compound. Composed of 2 or more like parts; e.g., a leaf with 2 or more leaflets or an ovary composed of 2 or more united carpels. Figures 7–8.

Corm. A short, thickened, vertical, underground stem, functioning as a storage or reproductive organ and either leafless or bearing poorly developed leaves.

Corolla. The inner series of floral organs when the perianth is differentiated into an outer and inner series. Figure 1.

Corona. A specialized structure present in some flowers between the corolla and the stamens and joined to one or the other.

Dehiscent. Splitting open at maturity in some predetermined fashion to discharge its contents as does a capsule or an anther.

Disc flower. One of the flowers with a tubular or trumpet-shaped corolla attached to the disc or central portion of the head; found in most Compositae. Figures 3 and 4.

Filament. The stalk of the stamen which supports the anther.
Figure 1.

Floral envelope. Same as the perianth.

Flower. The part of the plant which bears either the stamens or pistils, or both, and including any associated parts such as sepals and petals. Figures 1 and 2.

Fruit. The seed-bearing organ of the plant; more strictly speaking, the ripened ovary and other parts associated with it.

Habit. The general appearance of a plant.

Inflorescence. A flower cluster, including branches and bracts.

Involucral bract. A single bract of the involucre. Figure 3.

Involucre. A series of bracts closely associated with each other and with a flower or inflorescence; e.g., especially those bracts forming the outer portion of the head in the Compositae.

Joint. Same as node. Also, one of the sections of a dry indehiscent fruit resulting from crosswise fragmentation.

Keel. Any structure shaped like the keel of a boat, especially the 2 lower petals, taken together, of many leguminous flowers.

Leaf. The foliar organ of plants, normally bearing 1 or more buds in its axil. Figures 6–8.

Leaflet. One of the like parts of a compound leaf; the leaflets are attached to the central axis of the leaf or to the end of the petiole, not to the stem. Figures 7 and 8.

Ligulate flower. Same as a ray flower. Figures 3 and 5.

Lip. The enlarged or otherwise modified outer portion of 1 of the petals, especially in the Orchidaceae; in other families with bilabiate corollas, either the upper or lower half of the outer part of the corolla. Figure 2.

Lobe. One of the units of a simple leaf formed by partial division of the leaf blade; the outer part of the petal in a tubular flower that is not joined to the adjacent petals to form the tube.

Node. Refers to any of the points on a stem where 1 or more leaves or branches are attached; a joint.

Ovary. The enlarged, basal part of the pistil which encloses the ovules. Figure 1.

Ovule. The structure within the ovary that, upon fertilization of the egg, develops into the seed.

Palmate. Refers especially to compound leaves in which the 3 or more leaflets are all attached at the tip of the leaf stalk; also refers to leaves that are veined or lobed on this plan; i.e., are palmately veined or lobed, like the fingers on a hand. Figure 7.

Pedicel. The stalk of a single flower in an inflorescence.

Peduncle. The stalk of an inflorescence whether of an open or a condensed type such as that of the Compositae; also, the stalk of a single flower when it is the only one on the stem or branch of the stem.

Perennial. Lasting for more than 2 years.

Perfect. A flower with 1 or more functional stamens and pistils.

Perianth. The corolla and calyx taken together when both are present, or either of them when 1 (usually the corolla) is absent or when they are indistinguishable: the floral envelope. Figure 1.

Petal. One member of the corolla. Figure 2.

Petiole. The stalk of a leaf. Not always present. Figures 6–8.

Pinnate. Refers especially to compound leaves in which the 3 or more leaflets are attached at intervals along a central axis; also refers to leaves that are veined or lobed on this plan; i.e., are pinnately veined or lobed. Figure 8.

Pistil. The ovule-bearing organ, situated at the center of a flower, consisting of stigma, style (if present), and ovary. Figure 1.

Pistillate. Used with reference to flowers which have 1 or more functional pistils but have no functional stamens; a pistillate plant or inflorescence bears only pistillate flowers.

Raceme. An elongate, unbranched inflorescence bearing stalked flowers along its axis; the lowermost ones opening first, then the flowers opening progressively upward.

Ray flower. In many Compositae, a marginal flower of the head which has a strap-shaped corolla, when the disc flowers of the same head have tubular corollas. Same as ligulate flower. Figures 3 and 5.

Rhizome. An underground, often horizontal, branched or unbranched stem giving rise to above-ground stems and leaves from its upper part and to roots from its lower part. Distinguished from a root by its nodes, buds, and modified leaves, when present, and by its internal anatomy.

Rootstock. Same as rhizome.

Runner. An elongate, prostrate branch which roots at the nodes or tip; frequently gives rise to offsets, as in the strawberry. Same as a stolon.

Seed. A ripened ovule consisting of an embryonic plant and stored food materials either in the embryo or in specialized tissue outside the embryo, all encased in 1 or more protective layers, the seed coat.

Sepal. One member of the calyx. Figure 2.

Simple. Refers especially to leaves in which the blade is a single unit though it sometimes may be variously lobed or subdivided; however, the incisions or sinuses never reach the midrib. Figure 6.

Spathe. A large, usually solitary, often colored bract subtending and often enclosing an inflorescence; present in some monocot families.

Spike. An elongate, unbranched inflorescence bearing unstalked or very shortly stalked flowers along its axis, the lowermost opening first, then the flowers opening progressively upward. Sometimes applied to superficially similar structures.

Spur. A hollow, saclike projection usually from a petal or sepal which often produces nectar.

Stamen. One of the pollen-bearing organs of a flower consisting of an anther and, usually, a stalk, the filament. Figure 1.

Staminate. Used with reference to flowers that have 1 or more functional stamens but no functional pistil; a staminate plant or inflorescence bears only staminate flowers.

Staminode. A nonfunctional stamen, often lacking an anther and often highly modified in appearance, or any structure which because of its position in the flower is assumed to be a modified stamen.

Stem. The axis of the plant to which the leaves and flowers are attached.

Stemless. Lacking an above-ground stem; said of plants whose leaves and flowers arise from the crown at or near ground level; such plants may have underground stems of various kinds such as rhizomes, corms, or tubers.

Stigma. The part of the pistil that is specialized for the reception of pollen, usually distinguished by its sticky or minutely granular surface. Figure 1.

Stolon. Same as a runner.

Style. In many pistils, the prolonged, sometimes slender upper portion which separates the stigma from the ovary. Not always present. Figure 1.

Taproot. In many plants, the deep primary root which gives rise to smaller branch roots.

Tendril. A slender, sometimes branched organ which serves as the attachment of a vine or other weak-stemmed plant to its support.

Tuber. A short, thick, usually underground stem with 1 or more buds on its surface, which functions in food storage and in vegetative reproduction as, for example, a potato. The term sometimes is used for superficially similar storage organs formed from roots.

Tubercle. A stalkless swelling or enlargement, usually of different texture from the organ to which it is attached; it may be found, for example, on the back of the perianth valve in some *Rumex* species.

Tubular flower. A flower with a slender, tubelike corolla formed by the union of adjacent petals along their margins. In the Compositae, the same as disc flower. Figures 3 and 4.

Tufted. Occurring in a close group or clump.

Umbel. A more or less flat-topped inflorescence in which the branches of the inflorescence (when compound) or the stalks of individual flowers (when simple) are attached at the top of the peduncle, as the ribs of an umbrella.

Umbellet. One of the units of a compound umbel; the umbel of the second order.

Unisexual. Refers to a flower which has 1 or more functional pistils or stamens but never both; said of individual plants of some species which bear flowers of 1 or the other kind exclusively. A single plant of some species may, however, bear both staminate and pistillate flowers, or both unisexual and bisexual flowers.

Valve. One of 2 or more like parts of a compound structure such as 1 carpel of a capsular fruit or 1 of the dry, enlarged sepals enclosing the fruit in the sour dock.

Index to Plant Names

Index to Plant Names